THE ENVIRONMENTAL HANDBOOK

INTERNATIONAL PRECIOUS METALS INDUSTRY EMPHASIS

John E. Van Vlear, Esq., R.E.A.
Author

J.P. Rosso
Director of Publishing

Julia E. Kress, Esq.
Michael Paul Hutchins, Esq., P.E.
Contributing Authors

Gemini Industries, Inc.
Processors and Producers of Precious Metals
&
Brown, Pistone, Hurley & Van Vlear
A Professional Law Corporation

Publishers

Published by:

Gemini Industries, Inc.	Brown, Pistone, Hurley & Van Vlear
2311 S. Pullman St.	A Professional Law Corporation
Santa Ana, CA 92705	8001 Irvine Center Drive, #900
Phone: 714/250-4011	Irvine, CA 92718
	Phone: 714/727-0559

The Environmental Handbook is provided with the understanding that the authors and publishers (the "Book Team") are not hereby rendering legal, accounting, or other professional services. Before taking action based upon the contents, consult competent professionals for specific advice. The Book Team disclaims perceived or inferred: 1) representations or warranties, of any type, 2) conclusions as to the appropriateness of any course of action explored herein, and 3) endorsement of a particular company or individual. This handbook is not a publication of the International Precious Metals Institute. The opinions and views expressed herein are solely those of the authors. Except for the forms and information contained on the attached 3½ inch computer disk, no part of this book may be reproduced, stored in or introduced into a retrieval system, or transmitted, in any form or by any means (electronic, mechanical, photocopying, recording or otherwise) without the prior written permission of the publisher. *Adapted from a Declaration of Principles jointly adopted by a Committee of the American Bar Association and a Committee of Publishers.*

Acknowledgments: We wish to extend a special thanks to those people whose efforts made this book a reality. First is the staff of Brown, Pistone, Hurley & Van Vlear. Particularly important was the contribution of Denyse Hopkins (legal secretary and executive assistant to author Van Vlear) whose positive attitude and unique skills are invaluable. Thanks also to: Sue Greene (legal secretary), Laura Barron (legal secretary), Tina Ramirez (paralegal), and Jana Read (data coordinator). Finally, we express our appreciation to the others who added key elements to the effort: Howard Fine (Orange County Business Journal), David Bowls (law clerk), Ken Law (cover design, Lenac, Warford, Stone), Tim Crocker (Husky Bookprinters), and Georgieann Batley (executive secretary for the IPMI).

ISBN 0-9652553-0-1 (pbk)
Library of Congress Number: 96-76560

Copyright © 1996 All rights reserved
Gemini Industries, Inc. and Brown, Pistone, Hurley & Van Vlear

I dedicate *The Environmental Handbook* to my precious family:

Kimberley Ann, my bride and best friend for 16 years, whose love, patience, intellect, and enthusiasm bless my every step;

Victoria Susan, my older daughter, whose intensity and tenderness simultaneously challenge and melt me;

Megan Elizabeth, my younger daughter, in whose face I see all that is good in the world; and

Wilbur Louis (deceased) and Karen, my parents, whose values and endless support allowed me to grow personally and achieve professionally.

Thank you Lord.

John E. Van Vlear, Esq., R.E.A.
Author

SUMMARY CONTENTS

FORWARD. viii

CHAPTER 1: ENVIRONMENTAL CONTEXT. 1

CHAPTER 2: PRECIOUS METALS INDUSTRY. 3

CHAPTER 3: KEY U.S. OPERATIONAL LAWS. 13

CHAPTER 4: CERCLA (SUPERFUND). 29

CHAPTER 5: INTERNATIONAL REGULATION. 43

CHAPTER 6: STATE LAW CONCEPTS. 55

CHAPTER 7: CONTAMINATED PROPERTIES. 67

CHAPTER 8: ENVIRONMENTAL RISK MANAGEMENT. 77

CHAPTER 9: HAZARDOUS WASTE MINIMIZATION. 95

CHAPTER 10: TRANSPORTATION OF HAZARDOUS MATERIALS. 105

CHAPTER 11: EMERGENCY PREPAREDNESS. 115

CHAPTER 12: REFERENCE SOURCES. 145

APPENDICES

INDEX

BOOK TEAM PROFILES

DETAILED CONTENTS

FORWARD viii

CHAPTER 1
    ENVIRONMENTAL CONTEXT 1

CHAPTER 2
    PRECIOUS METALS INDUSTRY 3
    A.   Precious Metals 3
    B.   International Precious Metals Institute (IPMI) 5
    C.   Secondary Market 6
        1.   Precious Metals-Bearing Materials 6
        2.   Select Detailed Examples 8
            a.   Catalysts 8
            b.   Electronic Scrap 9
            c.   Jewelry 10

CHAPTER 3
    KEY U.S. OPERATIONAL LAWS 13
    A.   Resource Conservation and Recovery Act (RCRA) . . . 13
        1.   Regulation of Hazardous Waste 13
        2.   RCRA Exemption for Hazardous Waste
            Containing Precious Metals 17
    B.   Clean Water Act 22
    C.   Community Right-to-Know 23
        1.   Emergency Planning 24
        2.   Emergency Release Notification 24
        3.   Hazardous Chemical Inventory Reporting . . . 26
        4.   Toxic Chemical Release Reporting 26
        5.   Enforcement 27

CHAPTER 4
    CERCLA (SUPERFUND) 29
    A.   Elements of a CERCLA Case 30
        1.   Facility 30
        2.   Release of Hazardous Substance 31
        3.   N.C.P. Compliance and Causation 32
            a.   Consistency With the N.C.P. 32
            b.   Causation 34
        4.   Status As an Owner/Operator 34

B.		Select Key Issues	35
	1.	Petroleum Exclusion	35
	2.	Strict Liability Standard	35
	3.	No Right to Jury Trial	36
	4.	Section 113 v. Section 107 Debate	36
C.		Liability for Precious Metals Refinery Customers	37

CHAPTER 5

INTERNATIONAL REGULATION 43
A.		Basel Convention	43
	1.	Overview	43
	2.	Precious Metals under the Basel Convention	44
B.		Organization for Economic Cooperation & Development (OECD)	46
C.		CERCLA Concepts Internationally	47
	1.	Survey of Countries	47
	2.	British Environmental Act of 1995	48

CHAPTER 6

STATE LAW CONCEPTS 55
A.		California	55
	1.	Mine Cleanup Liability Protection	55
	2.	Lawrence Livermore National Laboratory Report	56
	3.	Single Agency Designation ("Certificate of Completion")	59
	4.	Nuisance	60
	5.	Trespass	62
B.		Pennsylvania	62
C.		New Jersey	63

CHAPTER 7

CONTAMINATED PROPERTIES 67
A.		Brownfields Redevelopment	67
B.		Facility Purchases/Acquisitions	68
	1.	Attorney Confidentiality	69
	2.	Description of Process	69
	3.	Managing Transactional Risks	70
C.		Environmental Consultants	71
	1.	The Selection Process	71
	2.	Where Cleanup Dollars Really Go	72
	3.	Developing a Short List	73
	4.	The Request for Proposal	73

iii

CHAPTER 8
    ENVIRONMENTAL RISK MANAGEMENT 77
    A.   Scope of Liability 77
        1.   The Corporate Veil 77
        2.   Shareholders 78
        3.   Officers and Directors 78
        4.   Parent Corporation and Subsidiaries 78
        5.   Successor Corporations 79
    B.   Risk Avoidance Strategies 79
        1.   Risk Management Program 79
        2.   Attorney Confidentiality Protection for Audits   80
        3.   Insurance 82
            a.   CGL Policies Covering Old Releases . 82
            b.   New Policies Available 84
            (1)   What to Look for When
                      Purchasing 85
            (2)   Pricing 88
        4.   Bankruptcy 89
            a.   Dischargeability 90
            b.   Automatic Stay 91
            c.   Abandonment of Contaminated
                    Property 92
            d.   Administrative Priority 92

CHAPTER 9
    HAZARDOUS WASTE MINIMIZATION 95
    A.   Getting Key Personnel Involved 96
    B.   Waste Minimization Group 96
    C.   Plan Objectives 97
    D.   Facility/Hazardous Waste Assessment 97
    E.   Prioritizing Wastes to Minimize 99
    F.   Reduction Alternatives 99
        1.   Changing Housekeeping or Inventory Controls   99
            a.   Areas for Waste Accumulations . . 100
            b.   Areas for Virgin Materials Storage . 100
            c.   Use of Current Inventory 100
            d.   Complete Usage Before Disposal . . 101
        2.   Substituting Less Hazardous/Nonhazardous
            Materials 101
        3.   Recycling 102
        4.   Eliminating Certain Processes 102

    G.   Feasibility Evaluation 102

    H.   Implementation/Maintenance 103

CHAPTER 10

TRANSPORTATION OF HAZARDOUS MATERIALS 105

    A.   Labeling 105

    B.   Packaging 106

    C.   Quantity Exceptions 108

    D.   Notification of Regulated Waste Activity 109

    E.   Required Documentation 109

         1.   Shipping Papers 109

         2.   Hazardous Waste Manifests 110

              a.   Required Information 111

              b.   Interstate Transportation 111

              c.   Copies 112

              d.   Generator Certification 112

         3.   Exception Report 113

         4.   Manifest Records Retention 113

CHAPTER 11

EMERGENCY PREPAREDNESS 115

    A.   Preparing for a Disaster 116

         1.   The Planning Team 116

         2.   Analyzing Hazards and Capabilities 116

              a.   Critical Products and Services 117

              b.   Internal Resources 117

              c.   External Resources 120

              d.   Vulnerability Assessment 120

         3.   The Response Plan 122

              a.   Basic Components 122

              b.   Media Relations 124

              c.   Personnel Considerations 125

              d.   Finalizing the Plan 126

         4.   Implementation 126

              a.   Training 126

              b.   Periodic Evaluation and Modification 127

    B.   Case Studies 128

         1.   Chemical Release, Union Carbide

              (Bhopal, India) 128

2.   Fires 130
     a.   Overview 130
     b.   Office Fires 131
     c.   Fire Prevention 132
3.   Floods 132
     a.   Risk Evaluation 133
     b.   Preparation and Recovery 133
     c.   Monsanto, 1993 Mississippi Flood (St. Louis, Missouri) 135
4.   Earthquakes 137
     a.   Special Risks 137
     b.   System Performance 140
     c.   Storage Tanks and Pipelines 141
     d.   Mitigation Programs 141
     e.   Nissan Emergency Response Plan (Carson, California) 141
     f.   Rocketdyne, 1994 Northridge Quake (Canoga Park, California) 143

CHAPTER 12
REFERENCE SOURCES 145
A.   Appendices on Computer Disk 145
B.   IPMI Library 145
C.   Internet Sites (Environmental/Precious Metals Industry) 145

APPENDICES

A   IPMI International Membership (List)
B   IPMI Membership Application (Form)
C   Biennial Waste Report (Form)
D   NCP Compliance (Checklist)
E   Preliminary Environmental Audit (Form)
F   Master Consulting Agreement (Example)
G   Phase I Consultant Selection (Checklist)
H   Assessing Current Facility Operations (Checklist)
I   Facility Information (Worksheet)
J   Characterizing Individual Waste Streams (Worksheet)
K   Description of Input Materials (Worksheet)
L   Options for Minimizing Hazardous Waste (Worksheet)
M   Specific Waste Minimization Option (Worksheet)
N   Feasibility (Worksheets)
O   Cost Estimation (Worksheets)

P C.F.R. Hazardous Materials (Table)
Q Hazardous Warning Label (Examples)
R Transportation Scenarios, Precious Metals (Example)
S Notification of Regulated Waste Activity (Form)
T Uniform Hazardous Waste Manifest (Form)
U Disaster Recovery Consultants (List)
V Planning Scenario, Newport-Inglewood Fault (Summary)
W Federal and State Emergency Management Agencies (List)
X Vulnerability Analysis (Worksheet)
Y Training and Drill Exercises (Worksheet)
Z Internet Addresses: Environmental/Precious Metals (List)

INDEX

BOOK TEAM PROFILES
  J.P. Rosso (Director of Publishing)
  Julia E. Kress, Esq. (Contributing Author)
  Michael Paul Hutchins, Esq., P.E., R.D.S.W. (Contributing Author)
  John E. Van Vlear, Esq., R.E.A. (Author)

FORWARD

Gemini Industries Inc., proud co-publisher of this book, recognizes the significance of furthering education and understanding all areas of environmental regulations. The company also believes in the relevance of making our industry and the public aware of the necessity for sane regulations and controls that help insure a clean environment for all. This awareness should then foster adherence to these laws.

We gratefully acknowledge the efforts and contributions made by the Author, Contributing Authors and the Director of Publishing in the writing and publication of this book.

Sebastian P. Musco
Chairman & CEO
Gemini Industries, Inc.

Our planet's environment provides the very foundation of the world in which we live. The precious metals industry has been instrumental in shaping that world in innumerable ways for thousands of years. As responsible members of both the world community and our own industry, it is our responsibility to take care of our world as we conduct our businesses into the future.

The people and companies who worked on this book believe very strongly that this responsibility for "stewardship" rests on all of our shoulders. To that end they have donated their money, their time and their talents to the development of this book. I thank all who contributed to this book for their tireless efforts and selfless contributions toward accomplishing this greater goal.

We sincerely hope that through our efforts, the world community as a whole and our industry in particular will both benefit through a more thorough understanding of the environmental rules and regulations that we must all follow.

J.P. Rosso
Director of Publishing

CHAPTER 1
ENVIRONMENTAL CONTEXT

This handbook reviews key U.S. and international environmental laws, identifies emerging trends, and analyzes how they combine to impact the profitability and operations of industry and precious metals companies. This endeavor also includes an analysis of proactive strategies such as risk management, waste minimization, and disaster preparedness.

The entire industrialized world now conducts business under intense environmental scrutiny. International, national, and local agencies regulate hazardous materials and wastes from generation through disposal. These regulations affect most segments of the global economy. The international precious metals industry is no exception.

In the United States, federal environmental laws are the product of three decades of legislation and rulemaking:

> A major catalyst for the birth of the environmental
> movement [in the late 1960's] was the transfer of political
> energy from the bitterly controversial and often violent civil
> rights and anti-Vietnam War movements to a movement that
> was clean, endured widespread support, and promised to
> transcend old ideological issues. Individual polluters made
> better devils than the very soul of America, which was at
> war with itself over civil rights and the Vietnam War.[1]

In 1969, the National Environmental Policy Act[2] placed restraints on governmental decision making for projects that might impact the environment. The 1970's witnessed a focus toward hazardous materials with

---

[1] Mattioni, <u>Pennsylvania Environmental Law Handbook</u>, Government Institutes, Inc., p. 1 (1994), quoting Frederick R. Anderson, <u>Environmental Protection, Law and Policy</u>, p. 6 (1984).

[2] 42 U.S.C. § 4321, *et. seq.*

the Clean Air Act,[3] the Water Pollution Control Act Amendments (commonly called the Clean Water Act),[4] and the Resource Conservation and Recovery Act ("RCRA").[5] Congress pursued cleanup of contaminated sites as a national priority through the Comprehensive Environmental Response, Compensation, and Liability Act of 1980 ("CERCLA" or "Superfund").[6] The U.S. enforces these statutes and resulting regulations through the Environmental Protection Agency ("EPA"). Additionally, prosecutors at the U.S. Attorney General's office and selected state agencies (who have been delegated those powers by the EPA) also undertake enforcement.

American states have enacted comprehensive environmental regulations and established state environmental agencies. These state laws are laboratories of innovation and diversity that are increasingly emerging as federal legislation.

Internationally, most countries have passed environmental laws regulating industrial operations, handling of contaminated properties, and related issues. Some of these laws parallel U.S. statues (e.g., CERCLA) while others fashion their own approaches. International conventions (e.g., Basel) and cooperative agreements directly affect the transboundary shipment of precious metals-bearing materials on the secondary market.

In the 1990's, a worldwide recession made businesses a top priority. Public opinion moved away from stringent environmental regulation to other issues. Budgetary constraints on regulators stalled the "staffing-up" of prior years. Technical expertise on environmental matters also matured. The environmental industry continued to consolidate and offer more competitive prices.[7] Because of factors such as these, three decades of increasing environmental regulation appears to have peaked.

---

[3] Id. at § 7401, *et. seq.*

[4] 33 U.S.C. §§ 1251-1376.

[5] 42 U.S.C. §§ 6901-6991(1976).

[6] Id. at §9600, *et. seq.*

[7] Environmental firms saw only a 7% growth in billings (gross revenue) for 1995. National and regional mergers and acquisitions continue to be a major driving force. This type of consolidation occurred in the American auto industry in the first half of the century (e.g., from a total of more than 100 domestic car manufacturers around 1920 to the present "Big 3") and the computer industry over the last decade.

CHAPTER 2
PRECIOUS METALS INDUSTRY

Companies in the international precious metals industry mine, extract, sample, analyze, refine, recover, mint, transport, and trade precious metals. The inherent value of precious metals-bearing materials fosters care in all phases of handling. However, in processing the metals, the industry employs a variety of chemicals (e.g., acids and cyanides), high voltage, large volumes of water, and high temperature combustion. The wide scope of these activities, and resulting waste streams, often trigger extensive environmental regulation.

A.   Precious Metals

Precious metals permeate human history. For example, the Bible mentions silver and its trading often, starting with Genesis.[8] Also, slag dumps in Asia Minor and on islands in the Aegean Sea show that man learned to separate silver from lead as early as 3000 B.C.[9] By contrast, other precious metals have more "recent" origin of only a few centuries: Ulloa in 1735 and Wood in 1741 discovered platinum in South America (although pre-Columbian Indians also appeared to have used it), while Wollaston in 1803 discovered palladium.[10]

Symbols that people used in ancient times still represent precious metals

---

[8] "Abram [Abraham] had become very wealthy in livestock and in <u>silver and gold</u>." Gen 13:2. "Abraham agreed to Ephron's terms and weighed out for him the price he had named in the hearing of the Hittites: four hundred shekels of <u>silver, according to the weight current among the merchants</u>." Gen 23:16 (emphasis added).

[9] Los Alamos National Laboratory, "Periodic Table," Internet address: http://www-c8.lanl.gov/infosys/html/periodic/periodic-main.html.

[10] <u>Id</u>.

3

today.[11] Long ago "educated" men linked the seven ancient metals (gold, silver, copper, iron, mercury, tin, and lead) with seven celestial bodies (respectively the Sun, Moon, Venus, Mars, Mercury, Jupiter, and Saturn). People used a symbol of the Sun (complete circle) for Gold since: 1) the sun was the dominant celestial body and gold has a similar status among metals; 2) gold appeared the same deep-glowing yellow color as the Sun; and 3) gold combines the characteristics of all other metals in harmonious balance (just like light from the Sun). The ancient people tied silver, which ranks second among the precious metals, to the moon (a semicircle or half-moon symbol). Silver's appearance strengthened the connection -- a shimmering glow but paler than gold. The industry still uses these symbols today.[12]

While the casual observer might consider many metals "precious," United States federal environmental law defines precious metals as:

> Gold, platinum, palladium and silver and their alloys. Any alloy containing 30 or greater percent by weight of precious metals is considered a precious metal.[13]

U.S. federal environmental law similarly characterizes precious metals recovery as including: "reclamation operations recovering gold, silver, platinum, palladium, the platinum group metals (iridium, osmium, rhodium, ruthenium), or any combination of the above."[14]

---

[11] Adapted from: "Ancient Signs in Cyber-Space," T-Time, p. 34-35 (No. 2, 1995). The origin of the symbols was the Ancient Greeks' idea that all substances derived from a common source and were strongly linked to the science of astronomy.

[12] For example, the Swedish precious metals company Trelleborg uses the ancient symbols as "icons" to assist viewers find information on their Internet homepage (http://www.trellgroup.se).

[13] 40 C.F.R. § 468.02(x), emphasis added.

[14] 50 Fed. Reg. 648 (Preamble, Jan. 4, 1985). In deciding not to expand this definition, the EPA noted: "The only comments disagreeing with this definition suggested (without explanation) that beryllium, germanium, gallium, and indium also be included. These metals are not ordinarily classified as precious, and commodity prices for these metals ordinarily are much lower than for the precious metals (in some cases several hundred times less)." Id.

B.   International Precious Metals Institute (IPMI)

The International Precious Metals Institute (IPMI) was founded in 1976. IPMI is a non-profit international organization headquartered in Allentown, Pennsylvania,[15] serving the technical, economic, and educational needs of the precious metals community. The organization is composed of miners, refiners, producers, users, research scientists, mercantilists, bankers, government representatives, and private individuals and companies. The IPMI is one of the largest, most prestigious precious metals associations in the world, having hundreds of active members, representing 50 countries. An *IPMI International Membership List* is attached as Appendix "A".

On a daily basis, the IPMI:

- Provides a forum for the exchange of information and technology.
- Seeks and promotes more efficient and environmentally sound use, reuse, and recycling of precious metals, from both primary and secondary sources.
- Conducts educational meetings and courses.
- Serves as a primary resource for information for the public, industry and government agencies worldwide.
- Recognizes excellence and achievement by means of awards to individuals and educational institutes.

The IPMI is active in furthering the interest of the precious metals industry worldwide. For example, during debates regarding the "Hazardous Wastes Burned in Boilers and Industrial Furnaces" regulation,[16] various drafts contained detailed permit and emission provisions which would have virtually destroyed certain segments of the secondary precious metals industry in the United States. However, after the IPMI intervened, the EPA specifically exempted the entire precious metals industry from the rule.[17] Similarly on

---

[15] IPMI, 4905 West Tilghman Street, Suite 160, Allentown, Pennsylvania 18104-9137, U.S.A. (telephone: 610/395-9700, fax: 610/395-5855).

[16] 40 C.F.R. § 266.100-112.

[17] Id. at § 266.100(f). While the EPA has suggested that it is not considering any changes to that rule, it may eventually review air emissions as the method of determining problems with industry furnace operations.

the international scene, the IPMI has been actively involved in the Basel Convention deliberations. At the 1995 first full meeting of the Technical Working Group in Germany, the IPMI persuaded the group to exclude many precious metals from the Basel Convention.

The IPMI annually hosts an International Precious Metals Conference. The meetings provide opportunities to attend interesting topical presentations by some fifty industry leaders and to establish dialogue with them and other registrants. Exhibits feature products and services provided by leading industry vendors. The Conference is held each June in a different venue.[18] The IPMI conference schedule is: San Francisco, California (1997); Toronto, Canada (1998); and Acapulco, Mexico (1999).

The IPMI offers several different classes of memberships, depending upon relationship to the industry and level of commitment.[19] An *IPMI Membership Application* is attached as Appendix "B."[20]

> C.   Secondary Market

The secondary market for precious metals-bearing materials is the reclamation and recycling trade. This market handles many industrial products that contain commercially viable amounts of precious metals.

> 1.   Precious Metals-Bearing Materials

The following materials on the secondary market often are worth recycling for their <u>gold</u> content:

---

[18] Past locations for the International Conference include: New York, Chicago, Providence (Rhode Island), San Francisco, Lake Tahoe (Nevada & California), Brussels (Belgium), Boston, Montreal (Canada), San Diego, Naples (Florida); Scottsdale (Arizona) and Newport Beach (California).

[19] IPMI company-type membership categories are: "Patron" ($2,000/yr.), "Sustaining" ($750/yr.), "Professional Association or Trade Organization" ($500/yr.), "Non-profit Institutes" ($150/yr.), and "Universities" ($75/yr.). Individual membership categories are "Qualified Member" ($90/yr.) and "Student" ($10/yr.).

[20] The Appendices are reproduced in computer format on the enclosed 3 ½ inch disk in a ready-to-use-and-print format.

Brazing alloys
Cladmetal parts
Contacts
Dental alloys
Dental scrap
Dental seeps/grindings
Diodes
Filled scrap
Filters-plating
Flakes
Flashings
Foil
Hooks-plating-nodules

Jewelry scrap
Jewelry sweeps/
  grindings
Paints and paste
Peelings
Placer
Gold
Plated parts-electrical
Plated wire
Powders
Printed circuit boards
  (with/without-parts)

Punchouts
Resins-plating
Salts-chemical
Sludges-plating
Solutions
Sponge
Tin lead alloys-
  (contaminated)
Transistors
Wiping rags
Wire

Silver has broad industrial applications and can be recycled from:

Anodes
Assemblies-electrical
Batteries
  (silver/copper)
  (silver/cadmium)
  (silver/zinc)
  (silver/magnesium)
Blanking scrap-
  punchings
Brazing alloys
Brushes-electric motors
Bullion
Chemical salts
Clad bi-metal parts
Coin silver
Contacts
Dental amalgam
Film

(industrial x-ray)
(medical x-ray)
(lithographic)
(photographic
  negatives)
Filters-plating
Flake-hyposolution
Hooks-plating-nodules
Jewelry sweeps
Paints-paste
Paper-reproduction
Plated
  (electrical)
  (electronic)
Plated serving pieces
Plated utensils
Plated wire

Powders-granulated
Punchouts
Relays-electrical
Resins
Silver lined bearings
  (diesel locomotives)
  (aircraft)
Sludges-
  plating/precipitates
Solutions-plating
Sterling silver
Tin lead alloys-
  (contaminated)
Turnings
Wave guides
Wiping rags

The following often contain enough __palladium__ to justify commercial reclamation:

Catalysts	Jewelry scrap/sweeps	Salts-chemical
Clad materials	Paste	Sludges
Contact points	Plated parts	Solutions
Dental alloys	Powders	Wire
Dental scraps/sweeps	Relays-electrical	

2.   Select Detailed Examples

a.   Catalysts

Petroleum and petrochemical refineries use all types of catalysts containing precious metals.[21] While catalysts are meant to enhance chemical reactions in the refinery without being directly consumed, decreased efficiency does require periodic replacement. Isomerization catalysts can last two years and reforming catalysts may last ten or twelve years. Each change-out represents millions of dollars in costs, including: fabrication (to manufacture the catalyst), precious metals (placed on the catalyst), contractors (change the catalyst out), lost production (while the unit is shut down), and reclamation (to reclaim the precious metals from the spent catalyst).

United States law regulates certain spent catalysts as a hazardous waste. This classification may apply, for example, if hazardous levels of base metals (e.g., copper) exceed federal or state regulatory toxicity thresholds (as determined by leachability tests) or because the catalyst is contaminated with wet hydrocarbon or other chemicals. Each catalyst user has a federal statutory obligation under RCRA to determine if its catalysts are a hazardous waste.[22] If the user decides they are, it must observe all applicable environmental regulations (e.g., for handling and transportation as respectively described in Chapters 3 and 7 of this Handbook).

---

[21] Adapted from: J.P. Rosso, "Maximize Precious-Metal Recovery from Spent Catalysts," Chemical Engineering Progress (December, 1992).

[22] 40 C.F.R. at § 262.11.

b.   Electronic Scrap

Recovery of precious metals from electronic scrap continues to grow, in part because of increasing supplies from: defective materials, excess inventories, and obsolescence of equipment (e.g., from computer and telecommunications industries and the military).[23] Electronic scrap is a "conglomeration of such things as circuit boards, components, integrated circuits, frames, relays, switches, thermostats, router dust, ceramic substrates, connectors, etc."[24] Recovery of precious metals from circuit boards continues to grow with each new wave of state-of-the-art computers (e.g., Pentium®, Pentium Pro®, 686-processors). With the large volume of printed circuit boards containing memory and peripheral chips, many refiners are now paying for pulled chips prior to processing the remainder of the boards for precious metals content.[25]

Circuit boards and other precious metal-bearing materials are commonly processed through devices such as shredders and mills (e.g., ball and hammer) to reduce their size. This process is necessary for accurate sampling and more economical packaging and transportation. Reclaimers ship the processed materials in boxes, bulkbags, supersacks, drums, and other similar containers. One can summarize this type of process as follows:

> Incoming materials are unloaded, inspected, weighed, and
> assigned a lot number. Processing begins by running the
> materials through one or more size reduction processes
> during which they take a representative sample (the percent
> sample varies with type and value of materials). Samples
> are assayed and the remainder of the lot is set aside until the
> company finalizes sample results. From arrival at a
> secondary facility until final reclamation of the metals, the

---

[23] Input into this section courtesy of: Steve Burns, ECS Refining (Greensboro, North Carolina, 910/545-0640).

[24] Yates (Sabin Metal Corp.), "Pyrometallurgical Processing of Electronic Scrap," IPMI 19th Annual Conference (Lake Tahoe, Nevada, 1995).

[25] Courtesy of: Don Walsh, BEHR Precious Metals, Inc. (Rockford, Illinois, 815/987-2680).

process normally takes between 8 to 12 weeks and can involve 15 to 20 steps.

When processing circuit boards and other electronic materials, reclaimers must take care to screen incoming items for components containing mercury or polychlorinated biphenyls (PCB's). They should take care to manage mercury and PCB components consistent with the applicable state and federal statutes[26] governing these materials.

At the request of the IPMI, the EPA issued an advisory that companies can handle recycled used circuit boards as scrap metal (as opposed to hazardous waste). The EPA has also issued a proposed rule that would exempt processed shredded circuit boards from hazardous waste regulation.

c.   Jewelry

Jewelry scrap (or "sweeps") consists of solid materials from shaping, polishing and burnishing operations, and has positive economic value due to its significant precious metals content. The regulators consider this material hazardous due to its metallic constituents only. Agencies distinguish jewelry sweeps from other operations in the jewelry industry that produce waste streams (e.g., plating, soldering, smelting and casting).

Jewelry waste generally is exempt from RCRA regulation under federal law. This occurs either because the waste does not exhibit toxicity, is exempt due to small quantities generated, or qualifies as exempt from full RCRA standards due to recycling or reclamation.

Some states, however, do regulate jewelry sweeps regardless of their RCRA status. For example, in California, for sweep volume greater than 5 gallons or fifty pounds, state hazardous waste laws apply (e.g., mandatory use of hazardous waste manifests and a registered transporter).[27] An internal agency memo, debating the issue of environmental regulation for the jewelry industry, provides:

---

[26] The Toxic Substances Control Act (TSCA), 15 U.S.C. § 2615, provides for penalties for violations of regulations promulgated thereunder. For example, 40 C.F.R. §761.60(a)(1) mandates disposal of PCB's at concentrations above 50 ppm (parts per million) by incinerator and 40 C.F.R. s 761.65(b)(1) makes illegal certain storage of PCB's greater than 50 ppm.

[27] California Health and Safety Code §§ 25160, 25163(c).

<u>Description of Issue</u>: Should the Department of Toxic Substances Control (DTSC) continue to regulate certain hazardous wastes generated by Jewelers which are known in the trade as "bench sweeps," as a fully regulated hazardous waste? . . .

<u>Circumstances Necessitating a Decision</u>: The intent of California's hazardous waste control laws is to protect public health and the environment from the threat posed by improper management of hazardous waste. In the case of jewelry waste (which is considered a hazardous waste due to the toxicity of its heavy metal content under federal and/or state criteria), the risk due to mismanagement of the waste stream is negligible, owing to the high economic value of the precious metal content of the waste. . . .

Imposition of restrictive management standards on generators and transporters of this waste may be burdensome and unnecessary, and provide little additional protective benefit to the public given the low risk posed by the waste. DTSC is compelled to take action to either provide a rationale and guidance for compliance with the current standards, or to revise the standards into a workable form. Failure to do so will cause continued uncertainty among the regulated community.

<u>Alternatives Available</u>:

1.   Do Nothing.

2.   Develop and promulgate a regulatory exemption for generators and transporters of jewelry wastes, under 22 C.C.R. chapter 13, article 4, to provide regulatory relief from the most burdensome of the state requirements (allow small quantity generators to transport w/out manifest and allow milkrun up to 1000 kg/mo for others).

3.   Develop and implement tiered permitting options
      for facilities managing this waste stream to provide
      for additional treatment capacity at both onsite and
      offsite facilities.

Public Information/Sensitivity Implications: This issue is
unlikely to be controversial or sensitive with the public at
large, or the environmental community. The jewelers and
transporters can be expected to support any effort to reduce
the level of regulatory burden they currently experience.[28]

In addition to the "sweeps" issue, the jewelry end of the precious metals
community faces other challenges. For example, processors must meet
federal Clean Water Act pretreatment standards, particularly when
discharging to municipal sewage systems. Jewelry businesses with inadequate
controls may run the risk of discharging excessive amounts of cyanide,
copper, lead, nickel, silver, and zinc.

---

[28] DTSC internal memo (1995).

CHAPTER 3
KEY U.S. OPERATIONAL LAWS

Complying with operational regulations is like driving a car on a crooked road.[29] More stringent environmental requirements equate to deepening "ditches" on the side of the road. Increased production is like a higher speed. As the speed goes up, so does the potential for driving off the road into the regulatory ditch. The trick is to have the proper equipment, training, and assistance to negotiate the road at virtually any speed.

A. Resource Conservation and Recovery Act (RCRA)

1. Regulation of Hazardous Waste

For American companies, including those in the precious metals industry, the principal federal statute regulating hazardous wastes is the Resource Conservation and Recovery Act ("RCRA").[30] In the early 1970's, Congress enacted the Clean Air Act and the Clean Water Act to address pollution of the nation's air and surface waters. However, these laws resulted in dramatically more solid waste. Legislators designed RCRA to remedy this regulatory void. Major provisions of RCRA include:

- Identification of wastes
- Management of hazardous waste
      a) at the point of generation
      b) during transportation
      c) that is to be recycled
- Regulation of treatment, storage, and disposal facilities (TSDF's)

Most of RCRA's requirements are implemented through EPA regulations.[31]

---

[29] Adapted from: "Logic and the Right Feeling for Environmental Protection," T-Time, p. 15 (No. 2, 1995).

[30] 42 U.S.C. §§ 6901-6991 (1976).

[31] The EPA's implementing regulations appear generally at 40 C.F.R. §§ 124, 260-272.

The EPA has now also granted many states the authority to locally administer RCRA.

RCRA establishes a comprehensive "cradle-to-grave" system for managing hazardous solid wastes[32] by regulating their generation, transportation, storage, and ultimate treatment or disposal. A solid waste is a "hazardous waste" if: (a) it is, or contains, a hazardous waste listed in the regulations,[33] or (b) it exhibits characteristics of ignitability, corrosivity, reactivity, and/or toxicity.[34] A person who generates a solid waste, has an <u>affirmative statutory burden</u> to determine if it is a hazardous waste.[35] If a solid waste is not a hazardous waste, then RCRA's hazardous waste provisions do <u>not</u> apply.

Small quantity generators of less than 100 kilograms of hazardous waste a month are conditionally exempt from RCRA regulation.[36] The quantity of hazardous waste generated can include hazardous waste produced by on-site treatment (as long as the pre-treatment hazardous waste is counted), or spent materials reclaimed on-site (again, as long as the spent material was originally counted).[37] Even small quantity generators, however, must have a RCRA permit or "interim status" (i.e., there has been an application submitted for a RCRA permit) if they generate: (a) one kilogram of acute hazardous waste[38] in a calendar month, or (b) a total of 100 kilograms of material resulting from the clean up of acute hazardous waste spills.[39]

---

[32] "A solid waste is any discarded material that is not excluded [by the regulations]." 40 C.F.R. § 261.2(a). "Materials are solid wastes if they are recycled-- or accumulated, stored, or treated before recycling ...." Id. at § 261.2(c).

[33] Id. at § 261.30-.34 (RCRA hazardous wastes lists).

[34] Id. at § 261.20-.24 set forth the tests for determining whether a solid waste exhibits any of these four key characteristics.

[35] Id. at § 262.11.

[36] Id. at § 261.5(a).

[37] Id. at § 261.5(d).

[38] For a list of acute hazardous waste, *see* Id. at §§ 261.31, 261.32 and 261.33(e).

[39] Id. at § 261.5(e).

By March 1 of each even-numbered year, all generators of hazardous waste must submit a *Biennial Waste Report* to the EPA regional administrator, a copy of which is attached as Appendix "C." In the report, the generator provides information on its status, on-site waste management practices, and waste minimization activity (including any changes in the volume and toxicity of the generator's waste compared with prior years). Biennial reporting requirements also apply to generators who treat, store, or dispose of hazardous waste on-site (i.e., do not transport off-site).

Any generator can accumulate hazardous wastes on-site for 90 days or less without having a RCRA permit or without obtaining *interim status*. This special exemption is only possible where the generator properly labels, contains, and documents the waste as being short-term.[40] Generators can accumulate hazardous waste on-site for up to 180 days, without a RCRA permit or *interim status*, if they generate less than 1,000 kilograms of such per month and never exceed 6,000 total kilograms.[41] The exemption applies only where the generator marks each container as being mid-term hazardous waste and where they have a proper emergency preparedness and prevention plan.[42]

An initial lack of criminal enforcement under RCRA led Congress to amend the statute in 1978, 1980, 1984, 1986 and 1988, in each instance significantly increasing the scope or severity of its criminal sanctions.[43] RCRA's criminal enforcement actions require that the offender act knowingly. RCRA provides for both individual and corporate criminal liability. The clear trend in federal criminal prosecutions is to target both corporations and their officers and agents.[44]

---

[40] Id. at §§ 262.34, 265.191-.195, 265.198-.199, 265.201, 265.200.

[41] Id. at § 262.34(d).

[42] Id. at § 265(c).

[43] Adapted from: Cooke, The Law of Hazardous Waste, supra., (1995).

[44] *See, e.g.*, United States v. McKiel, Cr. No. 89-24-N (D. Mass. June 29, 1989), 20 Env't Rep. (BNA) 520 (July 7, 1989) (corporate officials pleaded guilty to violations under RCRA and Clean Water Act); United States v. Biddle, Cr. No. 88-007R (N.D. Ga. Sept. 30, 1988), 19 Env't Rep. (BNA) 1186-87 (Oct. 14, 1988) (chemical brokerage firm and its president

It is a criminal violation to knowingly omit or falsify information in any RCRA application, permit, or manifest.[45] It is also a criminal violation to knowingly transport any hazardous waste without the required manifest.[46] RCRA makes it a crime to knowingly export a hazardous waste without the consent of the receiving country,[47] or in violation of any international agreement (between the U. S. and the government of the receiving country).[48]

The maximum fine for most RCRA violations is $50,000 per day of violation, with prison terms up to two years. Violations that "knowingly endanger" others carry maximum fines of $250,000 for individuals and $1,000,000 for corporations, with individual prison terms to a maximum of fifteen years.[49]

RCRA also has a citizen suit provision that allows any person to file a federal action against the same parties as the EPA can pursue.[50] The law requires that private parties give 90-day notice before filing suit (a requirement intended to allow the EPA to take action first if it so elects).[51] RCRA can be a particularly useful tool for a private plaintiff since, unlike CERCLA, it allows for the recovery of attorneys' fees[52] and does not contain a petroleum

_____

convicted of conspiracy to violate RCRA for knowing about transportation of hazardous wastes to an unpermitted facility, and knowing of storage and disposal of hazardous wastes without a permit).

[45] 42 U.S.C. § 6928(d)(3).

[46] Id. at § 6928(d)(5).

[47] Id. at § 6928(d)(6).

[48] Id. at § 6928(d)(6). *See, e.g.*, United States v. Franco, CR No. 90-352 (C.D. Cal. May 23, 1991), 1991 Haz. Waste Lit. Rep. (Andrews) 21025 (June 3, 1991) (defendant pleaded guilty to charges under RCRA that he illegally shipped waste to Mexico).

[49] 42 U.S.C. §6928(e).

[50] Id. at §6972(a)(1)(B).

[51] Id. at §6972(b)(2)(A).

[52] Id. at §6972(e).

exclusion.[53] However, a RCRA private action is limited to injunctive relief, i.e., the court cannot award damages or reimburse response costs.[54]

2. RCRA Exemption for Hazardous Waste Containing Precious Metals

Hazardous wastes containing economically viable amounts of precious metals are exempt from most, but not all, RCRA requirements. Valuable precious metals-bearing materials are typically recycled.[55] This practice fits squarely within the recycling mandates of RCRA, which one precious metals commentator summarized:

> In the beginning, the 1976 law drove most generators of
> hazardous waste to send hazardous waste materials to
> landfill. Since the spirit of the law was not to throw away
> the valuable resources, but to "C"onserve and "R"ecover
> them, the law was amended in 1984. The opportunity of
> land filling was greatly reduced. It is the goal of RCRA to
> recycle every hazardous waste.[56]

The EPA asserts regulatory authority over hazardous wastes which are recycled.[57] Since RCRA itself does not provide such express authority, the EPA looked to RCRA's purpose, language, and legislative history. For example, the EPA pointed to part of RCRA's legislative history suggesting that Congress viewed recycling as a method of managing solid waste. Based upon such interpretations, in 1980 the EPA promulgated standards regulating

---

[53] CERCLA cannot be utilized where there is only a release of "petroleum product" 42 U.S.C. § 9601(14).

[54] Meghrig v. KFC Western, Inc., 96 D.A.R. 3147 (March 20, 1996).

[55] "A material is 'recycled' if it is used, reused, or reclaimed." 40 C.F.R. § 261.1(c)(7).

[56] Duncan, "Is Hazardous Waste Edible?," IPMI 17th Annual Conference (June 1993, Rhode Island).

[57] This section includes material from: Susan M. Cooke, The Law of Hazardous Waste: Management, Cleanup, Liability, and Litigation (Matthew Bender, 1995).

a limited number of hazardous wastes during their transportation or storage prior to their being recycled.[58] In the 1984 Amendments to RCRA, Congress gave the EPA more direct statutory authority to regulate certain hazardous wastes which are to be recycled.[59] This authority recognizes the inherent difference between wastes to be recycled and those destined merely for disposal. As pointed out at an IPMI workshop:

> To suggest that recycling and disposal are significantly alike as to be regulated the same way, is equivalent to stating that a doctor and an undertaker are the same because they both deal with human bodies.[60]

The EPA has thus promulgated a special exemption for the process of reclaiming precious metal-containing wastes.[61] The financial value of this material ensures that generators, transporters, and reclaimers will prevent loss of the recyclable materials. The EPA summarizes:

> An examination of how these wastes are managed confirms that they are accorded special care due to their value. Management of these materials ordinarily is characterized by very careful handling from point of generation to point of recovery. Wastes containing these metals are at least placed in containers, and are sometimes neutralized, dried and shipped -- with armed guards -- in pouches to the reclaimer. Reclaimers and generators often enter into batch tolling agreements, requiring reclaimers to return the theoretically reclaimable amount of metal to the generator. For this purpose, wastes are typically assayed by both the generator and the reclaimer for precious metal content, and precautions are taken by the reclaimer to avoid loss. Wastes are containerized before reclamation; the Agency is

---

[58] 45 Fed. Reg. 33084, 33120 (Preamble, May 19, 1980).

[59] *See, e.g.,* 42 U.S.C. § 6935 (regarding used oil regulation).

[60] Ludo Van Hecke (Union Miniere s.a., Belgium), "Environmentally Sound Secondary Refining of Precious Metals ... From Cradle to Grave," IPMI Environmental Workshop (January 19-21, 1994, Arlington Virginia), quoting Dr. Herschel Cutler, Executive Director for the Institute of Scrap Recycling Industries.

[61] 50 Fed. Reg. 614, 648 (Preamble, Jan. 4, 1985).

not aware that open piles of impoundments are used for storage. Accumulation time by reclaimers also tends to be short (less than one month), because reclaimers often are required to return the reclaimed metal (or cash) to the generator within that time.[62]

While the EPA found justified at least a partial precious metals exemption from hazardous waste regulations, it also concluded:

> At the same time, <u>the Agency does not believe a complete exemption is warranted</u>. As pointed out in the proposal, individual precious metals operations have caused environmental harm, and some of the wastes being reclaimed -- such as spent cyanide solutions -- are very hazardous. In this regard, we note that some precious metal reclaimers themselves supported a partial, rather than total exemption. (*See, e.g.*, Comments of Engelhard Industries Division, July 30, 1983.)[63]

The resulting regulations provide that "recyclable materials"[64] (i.e., hazardous waste containing viable amounts of precious metals) are exempt from most, but not all, RCRA requirements:

> (a) [Applicability] The regulations of this subpart apply to recyclable materials that are reclaimed to recover economically significant amounts of gold, silver, platinum, palladium, iridium, osmium, rhodium, ruthenium, or any combination of these.
>
> (b) [RCRA Requirements Still Applicable] Persons who generate, transport, or store recyclable materials that are regulated under this subpart are subject to the following requirements:

---

[62] <u>Id</u>. (emphasis added).

[63] <u>Id</u>. (emphasis added).

[64] The EPA adopted the term "recyclable materials" in part to avoid any unnecessary stigmatization of hazardous wastes that can be put to beneficial use. 50 Fed. Reg. 614, 643 (Preamble, Jan. 4, 1985).

(1) [Notification of Regulated Activity]
Notification requirements under section 3010 of
RCRA;

(2) [Hazardous Wastes Manifests] Subpart B of part 262
(for generators), Sec. 263.20 and 263.21 (for transporters),
and Sec. 265.71 and 265.72 (for persons who store) of this
chapter;

(c) [No Speculative Accumulating] Persons who store
recycled materials that are regulated under this subpart must
keep the following records to document that they are not
accumulating these materials speculatively (as defined in
Sec. 261.1(c) of this chapter);
    (1) Records showing the volume of these materials
    stored at the beginning of the calendar year;
    (2) The amount of these materials generated or
    received during the calendar year; and
    (3) The amount of materials remaining at the end of
    the calendar year.

(d) [Full RCRA Regulation if Speculatively Accumulating]
Recyclable materials that are regulated under this subpart
that are accumulated speculatively (as defined in Sec.
261.1(c) of this chapter) are subject to all applicable
provisions of parts 262 through 265, 270 and 124 of this
chapter.[65]

The EPA's special requirements apply where reclaimers recover economically significant amounts of precious metals.[66] This requirement guards against a sham designation of "precious metals recycling operations." If precious metals are not present, or only present in non-viable trace amounts, then full RCRA requirements apply.[67] The EPA summarizes:

[T]he reclamation facility must be recovering economically significant amounts of precious metals from each waste for the waste to be conditionally exempt. For example, wastes

---

[65] 40 C.F.R. § 266.70.

[66] 40 C.F.R. § 266.70(a) (1987).

[67] 50 Fed. Reg. 648-649 (Preamble, Jan. 4, 1985).

for which small amounts of silver are recovered by a facility not ordinarily engaged in precious metal reclamation would not be exempt from regulation. Other factors indicating sham precious metal recycling are lack of strict accounting by either the generator or reclaimer of wastes to be reclaimed, storage [such as in open piles or impoundments] by either the generator or reclaimer not designed to protect wastes from release, payment to a reclaimer to accept wastes, or absence of efficient recovery equipment at the reclaimer's site. Generators or reclaimers engaged in this type of sham recycling without complying with RCRA regulations are, of course, managing hazardous wastes without complying with applicable regulatory standards[68] (emphasis added).

The EPA fully regulates resulting sludges and wastes from precious metals reclamation operations (e.g., high toxic metal and cyanide concentrations). As the EPA points out: "individual precious metal waste generators and reclaimers have the option of delisting the wastes from the reclamation process if they believe they are not hazardous."[69]

The EPA may also regulate individual precious metal recycling operations case-by-case.[70] If recyclable materials pose a threat to human health and the environment because of inadequate containment, or because of incompatible storage, then the facility may be subject to requirements developed especially for it. The EPA Regional Administrator's office must give notice stating the factual background and describing which of the hazardous waste standards they will require that the reclaimer meet. The notice becomes final in 30 days, unless any party requests a non-evidentiary, legislative-type hearing.

---

[68] Id.

[69] Id.

[70] Id. at §§ 266.40-.41.

After any such Regional Administrator final order, the applicant can appeal to the EPA Administrator, and then ultimately to the U.S. Court of Appeals.[71]

B.   Clean Water Act

The Federal Water Pollution Control Act Amendments of 1972, commonly called the Clean Water Act (CWA),[72] created a comprehensive national program to protect surface waters. The Act prohibits pollutant discharges unless authorized by a National Pollution Discharge Elimination System (NPDES)[73] permit, where the EPA allows point source discharges of pollutants.[74] Additionally, the CWA establishes pretreatment programs, imposing restrictions on discharges to publicly owned treatment works for any pollutant that would normally pass through the works untreated or interfere with its operation.[75] Upon the EPA's approval, states may establish and administer their own Equivalent Permit Program, which operate in lieu of the NPDES program.

The CWA provides civil, criminal, and administrative penalties for violations of its provisions. The CWA criminalizes a variety of "negligent" or "knowing" violations, such as falsification of information in record keeping or reporting documents, tampering with monitoring devices, and failures to notify the appropriate federal agency of reportable discharges of oil or hazardous substances.[76] The federal government has targeted numerous

---

[71] 50 Fed. Reg. 653 (Preamble, Jan. 4, 1985); 40 C.F.R. § 260.41(a) (1987).

[72] *See*, 33 U.S.C. §§ 1251-1376.

[73] Id. at § 1342.

[74] The term "pollutant" is defined broadly, and includes "dredged spoil, solid waste, incinerator residue, sewage, garbage, sewage sludge, munitions, chemical wastes, biological materials, radioactive materials, heat, wrecked or discarded equipment, rock, sand, cellar dirt and industrial, municipal, and agricultural waste discharged into water." Id. at § 1362(6).

[75] Id. at § 307(b).

[76] 33 U.S.C. § 1319(c)(4) and § 1321(b)(5).

22

corporate officers and individuals for prosecution.[77] For an analysis of how courts "pierce the corporate veil" to impose such liability, please refer to Chapter 8(A).

The CWA provides that convictions for negligent acts are punishable by a fine of not less than $2,500 nor more than $25,000 per day, imprisonment for not more than one year, or both. For knowing violations, the CWA establishes fines of not less than $5,000, nor more than $50,000 per day of violation, imprisonment for not more than three years, or both. Finally, the CWA subjects persons convicted of knowing endangerment to a fine of not more than $250,000, imprisonment for not more than fifteen years, or both. Knowing endangerment violations for organization subject the company to fines up to $1 million. [78]

C.   Community Right-to-Know

The goal of the federal Emergency Planning and Community Right-to-Know Act (EPCRA),[79] is to help communities better respond to chemical emergencies (in the wake of Union Carbide's disaster in Bhopal, India) and increase public's knowledge and access to information on the presence of hazardous chemicals in their communities and releases into the environment.[80]

---

[77] *See, e.g.,* United States v. Rutana, 932 F.2d 1155 6th Cir. 1991) (remanding case for re-sentencing of defendant on 18 counts of knowing discharge of pollutants into a public sewer system); United States v. Brittain, 931 F.2d 1413 (10th Cir. 1991) (affirming conviction of defendant on 18 counts of falsely reporting a material fact to government agency and two counts of discharging pollutants into waters of the United States); United States v. Boldt, 929 F.2d 35 (1st Cir. 1991) (affirming conviction and sentence of defendant on two counts relating to discharge of industrial wastewater to public sewer system).

[78]   33 U.S.C. § 1319(c).

[79]   42 U.S.C. §§ 11001-11050 (originally enacted 1986).

[80]   This section includes material from: Paul E. Hagen, "Federal Emergency Planning and Community Right-To-Know," IPMI Environmental Workshop (January 19-21, 1994, Arlington Virginia).

The four basic elements of the statute are:

- Emergency planning (§301)
- Emergency release notification (§304)
- Hazardous chemical inventory reporting (§§311-312)
- Toxic chemical release reporting (§313)

1.   Emergency Planning

The emergency planning element (EPCRA §301) has as its goal the development of state and local emergency response and preparedness capabilities through better coordination and planning. All state governors have now established State Emergency Response Commissions ("SERC's"), which in turn establish Local Emergency Planning Committees ("LEPC's").

All owners or operators of facilities, at which any extremely hazardous substance ("EHS") at or above the threshold planning quantity ("TPQ"), must notify the SERC[81] within 60 days of becoming subject to the requirements. [82] The EPA maintains a list of EHS's and the TPQ for each substance. [83] Facilities are to consider the total amount of EHS's present at any one time at the facility which are at concentrations greater than one percent by weight regardless of the location, number of containers, or method of storage. [84] The facilities must designate a representative to participate in local emergency planning and inform the LEPC. [85]

2.   Emergency Release Notification

The Emergency Notification aspects of the Community Right-to-Know law (EPCRA §304), provide a complementary (but independent) notification requirement beyond that found in other federal environmental laws (e.g., CERCLA). Owners or operators of a facility at which a hazardous substance is used, produced, or stored, must immediately notify the LEPC and SERC likely to be affected if there is an unpermitted release of a listed

---

[81] 42 U.S.C. § 11002.

[82] 40 C.F.R. § 355.30(b).

[83] Id. at § 355, Appendix A and B.

[84] Id. at § 355.30(a).

[85] 42 U.S.C. § 11003(d); 40 C.F.R. § 355.40.

hazardous substance that exceeds reportable quantities for the substance.[86] Notification can be by phone (with transportation incidents reported to "911") and must include the chemicals released, duration of release, and actions taken such as evacuations.

The following releases are exempt from the EPCRA §304 Emergency Notification Requirements:[87]

- Releases solely within the boundaries of a facility.[88]
- Federally permitted releases.
- Continuous and stable releases.
- Pesticide releases.
- Releases of certain naturally-occurring radio nuclides.

EPCRA § 304 also requires that as soon as practicable after such a release, the owner or operator of the facility shall provide a "written follow-up emergency notice" setting forth specific information concerning the release (e.g., actions taken to respond, advice on medical attention, etc.). [89]

The emergency notification provisions of EPCRA can be of particular concern for those in the precious metals industry given the potentially dangerous type of chemicals which may be present at precious metals recovery facilities (e.g., hydrochloric, nitric, and sulfuric acids). For example, cyanide is used for precious metals recovery from x-ray film and can result in a release of a solution of dissociated sodium cyanide (e.g., from cyanide process tanks) constituting a serious release for purposes of EPCRA notification. The listing for sodium cyanide includes that substance even when it is contained in manufacturing process wastes. If the percentage of cyanide in the solution attributable to sodium cyanide is known, a test for total cyanides may be used to establish a reportable quantity of sodium cyanide.

---

[86] 42 U.S.C. § 11004.

[87] 40 C.F.R. § 355.40(2).

[88] Note, CERCLA does not contain an on-site only release exemption from reporting to the National Response Center.

[89] 40 C.F.R. at § 355.40(b).

3.   Hazardous Chemical Inventory Reporting

The inventory reporting requirements of the Community Right-to-Know law (EPCRA §§ 311-312), requires owners and operators to notify state and local entities of the presence and amounts of hazardous chemicals at their facilities. Reporting under both sections is required for all hazardous substances present at any one time above 10,000 pounds (4,540 kgs) and for an EHS present at greater than 500 pounds (227 kgs) or the TPQ, whichever is lower.[90]

EPCRA §311 requires preparation or availability of Material Safety Data Sheets ("MSDS") for certain chemicals listed under the Occupational Safety and Health Act of 1970 ("OSHA").[91]   EPCRA §312 requires owners and operators to submit yearly an Emergency and Hazardous Chemical Inventory Form, referred to as Tier I.[92]   Based upon the Tier I submittal, or otherwise, the local agencies can request that a business submit a more detailed Tier II inventory form.[93]

4.   Toxic Chemical Release Reporting

EPCRA § 313 requires owners and operators of certain facilities to submit annually, to EPA and certain state officials, annual toxic chemical release inventory forms (Form R) for approximately 300 chemicals in 20 chemical categories.[94] Facilities covered are those with ten or more full-time employees falling within Standard Industrial Classification (SIC) Codes 20-39.[95] Facilities then must manufacture or process 25,000 pounds per year, or

---

[90] Id. at § 370.20(b)(1).

[91] 42 U.S.C. §11021.

[92] Id. at §11022.

[93] 40 C.F.R. § 370.25(c).

[94] 42 U.S.C. § 11023; 40 C.F.R. §372.65 (listing the chemicals). Information submitted under this section is used as a policy making tool by EPA and other governmental agencies.

[95] For example, the U.S. federal SIC for "Jewelry, Precious Metals" is Major Category 39 (#3911), Misc. Manufacturing Industry. 13 C.F.R. §121.601.

"otherwise use" 10,000 pounds per year, of the chemical to trigger the reporting requirement.[96]

5.   Enforcement

Under the EPCRA, the EPA may fine any person who knowingly and willfully fails to provide notice up to $25,000 for the first conviction, and up to $50,000 for a second or subsequent conviction. In addition, the government may imprison a person for not more than two years for the first conviction, or not more than five years for a second or subsequent conviction.[97] Penalties for EPCRA violations, however, are more typically monetary fines in the range of $5,000 for each chemical (i.e., for each failure to submit the usage Form R). If such a penalty is appealed, an administrative law judge, who should give full weight to the totality of the nature, circumstances, extent, and gravity of the violations, may reduce the base penalty for each of the violations (e.g., to $3,000 per violation). Adjustments to such base penalties are also possible if expenditures are made by the violator for environmentally beneficial purposes above and beyond those required by law.

While some cases have previously held that citizen suits can be brought for past violations even though the company is presently in compliance,[98] a late 1995 case held that citizens groups cannot sue for past violations of the EPCRA.[99] The citizens group in this later case brought suit against The Steel Company for alleged failures to inventory and file reports with the EPA from 1987 to 1995. Under the EPCRA, the citizens group was entitled to bring suit since the EPA did not prosecute within 60 days of the group's notice to the agency and The Steel Company. In a simple but ultimately effective maneuver, The Steel Company complied with the filing requirements before

---

[96] 40 C.F.R. §372.25.

[97] Id. at § 11045(b)(4).

[98] *E.g.*, Atlantic States v. Whiting Roll-up Door, 772 F. Supp. 745 (W.D. N.Y. 1991); Williams v. Leybold Technologies, Inc., 748 F. Supp. 765 (N.D. Cal. 1992).

[99] Citizens for a Better Environment v. The Steel Company, No. 95-4534, N.D. Ill (Dec. 19, 1995).

the 60-day notice period expired. The judge, citing the Sixth Circuit U.S. Court of Appeals,[100] found that this "fix" was sufficient and dismissed the case on the grounds that the EPCRA didn't allow for the citizens group's suit on what were now "historical" violations.

---

[100] Atlantic States Legal Foundation, Inc. v. United Musical Instruments U.S.A. Inc., 61 F.3d 473 (6th Cir. 1995).

CHAPTER 4
CERCLA (SUPERFUND)

The Comprehensive Environmental Response, Compensation, and Liability Act of 1980 ("CERCLA" or "Superfund"),[101] is the centerpiece of U.S. federal law related to contaminated property. Decades of releases, including innocent and sometimes well-intentioned disposal practices (such as pits, lagoons, and dry wells), created an American patchwork of contaminated sites. The public was outraged due to discoveries in the mid-1970's of Love Canal and other notorious hazardous waste dump sites. Congress responded by drafting legislation with global impacts.[102]

Under CERCLA, the EPA may either investigate and cleanup contaminated sites itself, or compel Potentially Responsible Parties (PRP's) to do so. The government funded the Superfund program with an $8.5 billion trust. Monies for the trust come from taxes on crude oil, chemical feedstocks, a corporate excise tax, and general federal revenues. The law also allows private parties to sue polluters using the same legal weapons available to the federal government.[103]

To help the EPA in carrying out its CERCLA responsibilities, the statute sets forth several reporting and record keeping requirements, and imposes criminal liability for violations. Criminal penalties range from a fine of less than $5,000 and imprisonment of not more than one year, to fines of $250,000 and imprisonment for five years. The most commonly prosecuted offense under CERCLA is failure to comply with the spill reporting

---

[101] 42 U.S.C. §9600, *et. seq.*

[102] One example of the global impact was on the venerable Lloyds of London. In the early 1990's, continuing CERCLA claims helped destroy Lloyds' ability to pay out on decades of reinsurance policies (bought by insurance companies). For the first time in their 300-year history, individual "members"(owners) of Lloyds paid huge personal contributions to keep the enterprise solvent.

[103] Id. at §9607.

requirements: operators of facilities must notify the National Response Center immediately upon discovering any unpermitted release of a reportable quantity of a hazardous substance.[104]

A.   Elements of a CERCLA Case

The federal government or private plaintiffs (collectively "plaintiff") in a CERCLA cost recovery action must prove at least four elements: (1) the contaminated site is a "facility," (2) there is a "release or threatened release" of a "hazardous substance," (3) plaintiff incurred "response costs," consistent with the National Contingency Plan (N.C.P.), because of the release or threatened release, and (4) the defendant is a liable party (e.g., an owner, an arranger, etc.) under the statute.[105]

1.   Facility

A plaintiff must initially prove that the waste disposal site is a "facility". CERCLA defines "facility" expansively:

> The term 'facility' means (A) any building, structure, equipment, pipe or pipeline (including any pipe into a sewer or publicly owned treatment works), well, pit, pond, lagoon, impoundment, ditch, landfill, storage container, motor vehicle, rolling stock, or aircraft, or (B) any site where a hazardous substance has been deposited, stored, disposed of, or placed, or otherwise come to be located; but does not include any consumer product in consumer use or any vessel.[106]

The CERCLA definition of "facility" is given broad interpretation:

> (T)he legislative history makes clear Congress' intent to address the problem of hazardous wastes rather than merely a particular category of disposal sites. Indeed, it appears that Congress sought to deal with every conceivable area

---

[104] Id. at §9603.

[105] Ascon Properties, Inc. v. Mobil Oil Co., 866 F.2d 1149, 1152-3 (9th Cir. 1989).

[106] 42 U.S.C. § 9601(9) (emphasis added).

where hazardous substances come to be located ....[107]

2.   Release of Hazardous Substance

The plaintiff must next show a release or threatened release of hazardous substances. CERCLA uses "release" very expansively:

> The term "release" means any spilling, leaking, pumping, pouring, emitting, emptying, discharging, injecting, escaping, leaching, dumping, or disposing into the environment . . . .[108]

CERCLA uses an umbrella definition of "hazardous substance" which encompasses chemical listings from many sources.[109] CERCLA specifically lists silver as a hazardous substance. CERCLA also identifies as hazardous substances commonly found in secondary precious metal-bearing material, including:[110]

---

[107] State of N.Y. v. General Electric Co., 592 F.Supp. 291, 296 (N.D.N.Y. 1984) (drag strip to which contaminated oil had been applied is a 'facility') (emphasis added).

[108] 42 U.S.C. § 9601(22).

[109] The term 'hazardous substance' means (A) any substance designated pursuant to §1321(b)(2)(A) of Title 33, (B) any element, compound, mixture, solution or substance designated pursuant to §9602 of this title, (C) any hazardous waste having the characteristics identified under or listed pursuant to §3001 of the Solid Waste Disposal Act [42 U.S.C.A. §6921 . . ., (D) any toxic pollutant listed under §1317(a) of Title 33, (E) any hazardous pollutant listed under §112 of the Clean Air Act [42 U.S.C.A. §7412], and any imminently hazardous chemical substance or mixture with respect to which the Administrator has taken action pursuant to §2606 of Title 15.   Id. at §9601(14).

[110] Bullock, John C. (Handy & Harmon), "Environmental Decision-Making: Closing the Plant Door as a Response to Hazardous Air Pollution Standards," IPMI 14th Annual International Conference (June, 1990, San Diego, California);   Bullock, John C., "Superfund Liability of Precious Metal Refinery Customers, " IPMI Environmental Workshop (January 19-21,

beryllium	cyanides	mercury
cadmium	lead	selenium
chromium	nickel	sulfuric acid
copper	nitric acid	zinc

3.   N.C.P. Compliance and Causation

The plaintiff must incur response costs[111] because of the release or threatened release, consistent with the National Contingency Plan.[112] The N.C.P. has specific rules which a responding party must comply with to earn the right to sue under CERCLA. If response costs are only for preliminary investigation or monitoring, there is no N.C.P. compliance requirement.[113]

a.   Consistency With the N.C.P.

Courts evaluate consistency with the N.C.P. under a relaxed "substantial compliance" standard:

> For the purposes of cost recovery under §107(a)(4)(B) of CERCLA: A private party response action will be considered "consistent with the N.C.P." if the action, when evaluated as whole, is in substantial compliance with the applicable requirements in paragraphs (c)(5) and (6) of this section, and results in a CERCLA-quality cleanup . . . . .[114]

1994, Arlington Virginia).

[111] The terms 'respond' or 'response' mean: remove, removal, remedy, and remedial action. 42 U.S.C. § 9601(25).

[112] Id. at §9607(a)(4), (a)(4)(B).

[113] Donahey v. Bogle, 987 F.2d 1250 (6th Cir. 1993) (consistency with N.C.P. not necessary for recovery of monitoring investigative costs); Carlyle Piermont Corp. v. Federal Paper Bd. Co., 742 F.Supp. 814 (S.D.N.Y. 1990) (consistency with N.C.P. not necessary for recovery of monitoring investigative costs).

[114] 40 C.F.R. §300.700 (c)(3). While the N.C.P. used to apply a "strict" compliance standard, the EPA softened the revised N.C.P. to impose only "substantial" compliance.

The N.C.P. also provides that responding parties must always conduct a "baseline risk assessment."[115] While this requirement is mandatory, it is often tough deciding the proper extent of the risk assessment. In some situations, an inexpensive risk assessment may comply; in others, the risk assessment might have to be extensive to achieve N.C.P. compliance.

Another key requirement of the N.C.P. is a feasibility study ("FS").[116] The feasibility study ensures that decision-makers develop and evaluate appropriate remedial alternatives before selection. The FS must include a "no-action" alternative. Failure to do so opens a plaintiff to defendants' attacks on the basis that plaintiff should have just left the contamination in place. Feasibility studies should expressly list the required evaluation factors:

- Overall protection of human health and the environment
- Compliance with federal/state ARAR's (applicable or relevant and appropriate requirements)
- Long-term effectiveness
- Reduction of toxicity, mobility or volume through treatment
- Short-term effectiveness
- Implementability
- Costs
- State acceptance
- Community acceptance

Finally, the plaintiff <u>must</u> provide an opportunity for public comment concerning the selection of a response action. The EPA summarizes:

> Public participation is an important component of a
> CERCLA-quality cleanup and of consistency within the
> N.C.P. The public - both PRP's and concerned citizens -
> have a strong interest in participating in cleanup decisions
> that may affect them, and their involvement helps ensure
> that these cleanups - which are performed without
> governmental supervision - are carried out in an
> environmentally sound manner. Thus, the EPA has decided

---

[115] <u>Id</u>. at § 300.430(d)(4).

[116] <u>Id</u>. at § 300.430(e).

that providing public participation opportunities <u>should be a condition for cost recovery under CERCLA.</u>[117]

The *N.C.P. Compliance Checklist*, attached as Appendix "D," helps identify several key N.C.P. "trip-wires" which may snare unsuspecting responding parties. Failures to comply with the N.C.P. can be fatal to a CERCLA lawsuit.

b. Causation

The EPA has relaxed the causation standard under CERCLA:

> CERCLA does not set out an express standard of causation. Nevertheless (the) structure of CERCLA and its legislative history <u>make it clear that traditional tort notions, such as proximate cause, do not apply.</u> Moreover, the practical limits on analytic techniques argue for a weaker causation standard. . . . Thus, CERCLA <u>requires only a relaxed standard of causation.</u>[118]

4. Status As an Owner/Operator

Finally, the defendant must fit into one of the following categories:

• Present owner/operator[119]

---

[117] N.C.P. Comments, <u>Federal Register</u>, p.8795 (March 8, 1990), emphasis added.

[118] <u>United States v. Bliss</u>, 667 F.Supp. 1298, 1309 (E.D. Mo. 1987) (emphasis added).

[119] The term "owner or operator" means . . . (ii) in the case of an onshore facility . . . any person owning or operating such facility ... <u>Id</u>. at §9601(20)A. To further specify the meaning of "operator," courts look to whether the entity in question had the authority to control the area where the hazardous substances are located. *See, e.g.,* <u>Nurad, Inc., v. William E. Hooper & Sons, Co.</u>, 966 F.2d 837, 842 (4th Cir. 1992); <u>Long Beach Unified School District v. Godwin</u>, 32 F.3d 1364, 1367 (9th Cir. 1994); *See also,* <u>Kaiser Aluminum & Chemical Corp. v. Catellus Dev. Corp.</u>, 976 F.2d 1338, 1341 (9th Cir. 1992) following <u>Nurad</u>.

- Past owner/operator[120]
- Arranger for disposal
- Transporter

B.   Select Key Issues

1.   Petroleum Exclusion

When Congress was debating the original passage of CERCLA, two factors combined to exclude petroleum releases. First, the American oil industry mounted an intense lobbying effort. Second, the legislators decided the cleanup of all gas station sites in the country would be too expensive. Thus, the final version of CERCLA excluded petroleum releases from its "hazardous substances" definition:

> The term [hazardous substances] does not include petroleum, including crude oil or any fraction thereof which is not otherwise specifically listed or designated as a hazardous substance under subparagraphs (A) through (F) of this paragraph, and the term does not include natural gas, natural gas liquids, liquefied natural gas, synthetic gas usable for fuel (or mixtures of natural gas and such synthetic gas).[121]

2.   Strict Liability Standard

Strict liability means that liability attaches regardless of fault. This old English notion started with unpunished harm from the maintaining of wild animals and the handling of explosives. Defendants in England escaped liability by saying they had done everything a prudent person would do under the same or similar circumstances (a negligence standard). The Courts of Equity imposed liability anyway because the activity was so inherently dangerous that by simply undertaking it the defendants became responsible

---

[120]   "[A]ny person who <u>at the time of disposal</u> of any hazardous substance owned or operated any facility at which such hazardous substances were disposed of." 42 U.S.C. § 9607(A)(2)(emphasis added).

[121]   <u>Id.</u> at § 9601(14).

for all damages caused (even if they had acted prudently).

While CERCLA itself is silent on the issue, the courts have readily concluded that strict liability applies to cost recovery actions.[122] This means that even if a given disposal practice was prudent and common years ago, the company is liable for all response costs regardless of fault. This policy represents a political decision by Congress to make "polluters pay" instead of the U.S. taxpayers.

3. No Right to Jury Trial

Since cost recovery actions are "equitable" in nature, there is no right to a jury under CERCLA.[123] This factor can be important in determining litigation strategy. For example, many cases have both state law claims (e.g., nuisance), where there is a right to a jury, and CERCLA claims. If there is a sympathetic party on the other side of a case (e.g., individuals, even if wealthy), corporate plaintiffs may waive a jury. By having the judge determine all issues, the corporation hopes to neutralize the sympathy that typically attached to the "little guy" in such trials.

4. Section 113 v. Section 107 Debate

Federal courts across the U.S. are debating whether private party plaintiffs may bring a CERCLA action under § 107, the traditional joint and several liability approach,[124] or whether they are limited to a § 113 contribution

---

[122] *See, e.g.,* Dedham Water Co. v. Cumberland Farms Dairy, 889 F.2d 1146, 1152-53 (1st Cir. 1989); State of N.Y. v. Shore Realty Corp., 759 F.2d 1032, 1044 (2d Cir. 1985); United States v. Stringfellow, 1986 Haz. Waste Litig. Rep. 9809 (C.D. Cal. 1986).

[123] *See, e.g.,* Mardan Corp. v. C.G.C. Music, Ltd., 600 F.Supp. 1049, 1056 n.9 (D. Ariz 1984), *aff'd*, 804 F.2d 1454 (9th Cir. 1986) (a CERCLA section 107 claim is equitable in nature); Ross v. Bernhard, 396 U.S. 531, 90 S. Ct. 733, 24 L. Ed. 2d 729 (1970) (for claims which are equitable in nature, there is no Seventh Amendment right to a jury trial).

[124] Under a joint and several liability scheme, a one percent contributor may become liable for the entire cleanup if the other contributors are insolvent or cannot be found.

claim.[125] The impact of eliminating joint and several liability can be huge, especially where the parties involved represent only a fraction of the contributors. In just such a case, the author's law firm successfully limited a plaintiff to a § 113 claim. The firm persuaded Judge Alice Marie Stotler to put aside a recent opposite ruling by the District's presiding judge in another case. Judge Stotler respectfully held:

> One court in this district has held that a responsible party such as Dyer may bring an action under CERCLA §107 as well as CERCLA §113. See, Transportation Leasing Co. v. State of California (Cal Trans), 861 F. Supp. 931, 937-38 (C.D. Cal. 1993).   . . .
>
> The Court *respectfully parts company* with Transportation Leasing and holds that Dyer, as a responsible party, is limited to a §113 contribution action and may not bring a cost recovery action under §107.[126]

Action by the U.S. Supreme Court, or a change in the legislation, is necessary to avoid such radically different judicial opinions.

C.   Liability for Precious Metals Refinery Customers

The customers of precious metal recycling companies have significant liability

---

[125] Under a contribution claim, a defendant would only have to pay its fair share of the response costs. *See, e.g.*, United Technologies Corp. v. Browning-Ferris Indus., Inc., 33 F.3d 96, 98-101 (1st Cir. 1994); Akso Coatings, Inc. v. Aigner Corp., 30 F.3d 761, 764-65 (7th Cir. 1994); United States v. Colorado & Eastern Railroad Co., 50 F.3d 1530, 1536 (10th Cir. 1995).

[126] Stotler, Judge Alice Marie, Minute Order, Dyer Business Associates v. Dinamation International Corp., et. al., United States District Court, Central District of California, SA CV 92-001 (July 31, 1995). This decision received national press, *see e.g.*, "Section 107 v. Section 113 Claims: PRP Can Only Pursue Contribution Claim Action Against Other PRPs; U.S. Judge in California Notes Split Among Courts on This Issue, Sides with Majority," Mealey's Superfund Reports, Vol 8, Issue 11 (Sept. 13, 1995).

exposure if they choose an unqualified refiner. As John Bullock, General Counsel for Handy & Harman, stated to the IPMI several years ago:

> If a jewelry manufacturer spills a gold cyanide plating bath onto the ground, is the supplier of that bath responsible for the environmental damage? No. When the jewelry manufacturer sends that gold cyanide plating bath back for recovery of the gold, is it legally responsible for the environmental damage at the precious metal refinery? Yes. And not just for damage associated with that shipment of plating bath, but for all environmental contamination at the site. How can this be? In a word, Superfund [CERCLA].[127]

Reclamation is not equivalent to "disposal," nor are precious metal-bearing materials generally viewed as wastes. However, four basic arguments explain how precious metal refineries and their customers may fall within the scope of CERCLA. As John Bullock summarized:[128]

> 1) <u>Precious metal-bearing material is waste.</u> The EPA once took the position that precious metal-bearing material, including cyanide baths and sludges, was never discarded and thus was not waste. Since 1985, however, the EPA has asserted that some material is a waste even if it is <u>never</u> discarded. Significantly for metal reclamation, the EPA asserted that all scrap metal is waste. The EPA also stated that some precious metal-bearing material is hazardous waste. Cyanide plating baths and spent solvents, for example, are listed hazardous wastes, notwithstanding that they contain significant amounts of precious metal. Although the EPA has not regulated precious metal refining to the same extent as hazardous waste disposal, refining operations for hazardous waste are within the definition of treatment, i.e., "a method, technique, or process designed to change the physical, chemical, or biological character or composition of any hazardous waste to render such waste . . amenable for recovery." Thus, the EPA will consider a

---

[127] Bullock, John C., "Superfund Liability of Precious Metal Refinery Customers," IPMI 13th Annual Conference, Newport, Rhode Island (October 1989).

[128] <u>Id</u>.

person who arranges for precious metal refining of hazardous waste to have arranged for its treatment, and to be liable under Superfund (emphasis added).

2) Precious metal refining includes waste disposal. Most precious metal-bearing secondary material contains more than precious metal, and the other constituents are unwanted by both the refinery and the customer. An arrangement for refining will include terms for recovery of any precious metal content, but not of base metals and other constituents. Processing of a jeweler's gold cyanide plating bath, for example, typically involves precipitation of the gold, leaving a residual valueless cyanide waste to be disposed of by the refiner. The EPA considers such non-recovered constituents to be wastes, and the refining arrangement, which includes a charge for all processing, to include such cyanide waste disposal. Thus, even though the unprocessed material is a valuable material overall, in most precious metal refining the disposal theory of CERCLA liability has force.

3) CERCLA liability is not related to waste. The EPA asserts that CERCLA imposes liability for "disposal or treatment . . .of hazardous substances," not hazardous wastes. Thus even though disposal and treatment are defined in terms of waste, the material involved need not be waste.   . . .

The EPA has claimed CERCLA liability under this argument in a case directly involving precious metal reclamation. In United States v. Bourdeaudhui,[129] a case brought in 1988 in the United States District Court in Connecticut, the EPA sought to recover its costs of cleaning up two dental amalgam refining sites. The EPA asserted that persons who arranged for dental amalgam to be refined, including individual dentists and brokers, were liable under CERCLA as having arranged for disposal or treatment.

---

[129]   Civil Action No. H-88-354, United States District Court, District of Connecticut.

Defendants' assertions that dental amalgam was not a hazardous waste was considered by the EPA to be irrelevant, and the EPA asserted as a basis for liability that:

> "Silver and mercury are principal constituents of silver amalgam and are both hazardous substances under CERCLA. This process resulted in the release of mercury and the contamination of the site." . . .

The government position in Bourdeaudhui is particularly revealing, because all the CERCLA hazardous substances involved in that case, silver and mercury, were intended for complete recovery. No actual disposal of any hazardous substance was intended by any party involved in the case. The EPA position is thus that an arrangement for reclamation of valuable precious metal-bearing material . . . brings with it Superfund liability for contamination of the refinery.

4) A refinery customer is responsible for waste generated in a contract refining process. A recent case involves still another theory of Superfund liability, and a suggestion of liability beyond the refinery site itself. In United States v. ACETO Agricultural Chemicals, [130] under circumstances similar to toll-processed precious metal refining, the EPA asserted that a person may be responsible for pollution caused by waste generated and disposed of by another person. . . . When the Aidex facility was found to be contaminated, and Aidex went bankrupt, the EPA sought cost recovery of cleanup costs from the chemical suppliers.

These suppliers asserted that they had supplied product, and not waste, and that there was no element of disposal in their dealings with Aidex. The EPA disagreed, asserting that the chemical suppliers had not merely sold products, but retained title to such chemicals through Aidex's processing. . . . The chemical suppliers were responsible for the chemical waste generated by Aidex, for contamination of the Aidex facility resulting from that waste, and for the

---

[130] 872 F. 2d 1373, 29 ERC 1529 (8th Cir. 1989).

costs of cleaning up the facility.

Is that the limit of Superfund liability under this theory? In the <u>ACETO</u> case a contract chemical company processor mismanaged the waste it generated, contaminating its own facility, and its chemical suppliers were held to be responsible for that contamination. But if the suppliers are responsible for waste generated in the course of contract services, will the suppliers not be responsible for that same waste "from cradle to grave?" If the contract chemical processor disposed of the waste at an offsite facility, would the suppliers then incur Superfund liability at that facility? Although the case itself does not say, the theory makes such a conclusion a possibility.

This last tactic is an example of CERCLA's broad "deep pockets" framework that has caused business outrage and has prompted legislative reform efforts.

CHAPTER 5
INTERNATIONAL REGULATION

A.   Basel Convention

1.   Overview

In the late 1980's, news stories reported large shipments of municipal and industrial wastes from the United States and Europe to developing countries.[131] Some ships sailed from port to port, unable to unload cargos of waste. The "Morbro 4000," a garbage barge, was one particularly famous example. The ship traveled for six months in 1987 before returning its load to its origin in New York. Such shipments became media symbols of egregious disregard for people and the environment.

In 1989, the United Nations Environment Programme led various countries to draft an international agreement entitled the <u>Basel Convention on the Control of Transboundary Movements of Hazardous Wastes and Their Disposal</u> ("Basel" or "Basel Convention"). One commentator opined:

> [T]his Convention was signed in touchy environmental circumstances, i.e., at a moment when a series of "waste scandals" were making the first pages of all medias throughout the world. The result was this well-known, badly-coordinated environmental bottleneck, in which no account at all had been taken of the economic reality.[132]

The Basel Convention requires that when someone in one country wants to ship "hazardous waste" to another, they must notify the receiving government

---

[131]   Adapted from: Petrikin, "Halting the Trade in Recyclable Wastes Will Hurt Developing Countries," <u>Environmental Justice</u>, pp. 108-109, 112 (1994).

[132]   Dr. Arlette Shagarofsky-Tummers (Deputy Secretary-General, Eurometaux), "The Basel Convention--The View from Europe," IPMI 15th Annual International Conference (June, 1991, Naples, Florida).

and obtain written permission. If a country does not want to import the waste, it can deny importation for any reason. The drafters originally intended the Basel Convention to be a safeguard to assure that the imported materials met reasonable specifications (e.g., is not simply garbage). They also wanted countries to return materials if misrepresented and foster environmentally sound management of any facilities using the secondary raw materials.

2.   Precious Metals under the Basel Convention

The Basel Convention turned out to be an approach with the potential to block trade in secondary materials between the Organization for Economic Co-Operation and Development ("OECD") and the rest of the world, including fast growing, modern nations in the Pacific Rim and South America. Basel continues to offer the possibility of creating additional burdens on trade within the OECD and within the fledgling European Union ("EU").

Initially, the drafters decided to include within the Basel Convention all "operations which may lead to resource recovery, recycling, reclamation, direct re-use or alternative uses." In short, they grouped some of the most valuable materials on earth into the same category as municipal garbage. They proposed classifying secondary materials as waste unless they were free of certain constituents and passed certain tests for hazardous components.

Among the constituents which brought secondary materials under Basel were lead, inorganic cyanides, copper compounds, zinc compounds, and a wide list of other materials. The list of hazardous characteristics includes poisonous (acute), toxic (delayed or chronic), eco-toxic, and "capable, by any means, after disposal, of yielding another material, e.g., leachate, which possesses any of the characteristics above." The Convention enumerates no specific tests in this area and it lays out no threshold amounts of hazardous constituents. Thus, it seems that a molecule of a hazardous characteristic would bring a ton of otherwise acceptable materials under Basel (with the burden being on the exporter to prove otherwise).

At the first meeting of the Basel parties, they advanced the proposition that giving nations the right to refuse any unwanted import was not an adequate protection. They argued that some nations were too corrupt, or too ignorant, to protect themselves. They proposed that Basel should ban the export of Basel "wastes" from the OECD to all other nations. Under Basel terms, this could have banned all secondary market precious metals-bearing materials. Leading the fight for these provisions were many of the nations within the

44

EU considered "greener than green." Others viewed Basel as a means of building favorable trade barriers.

At the third meeting of the Basel parties, they adopted a modified ban. Two "bright spots" emerged. First, there was a plan under which countries can seek the approval of the Convention to opt out of the ban. Second, the Technical Working Group was directed to come up with a report for the fourth meeting of the parties to better determine what the Convention covers and what it does not. Many people expect that the Technical Working Group report will eventually become the basis for revisions to the OECD agreement and for the EU internal regulations.

Because of the Basel Convention's growing importance, the IPMI has actively participated in the debate. At the first full meeting of the Technical Working Group in Germany in December 1995, the IPMI was able to get the group to put many precious metals into a Basel excluded category. However, there were many caveats, and some secondary precious metals-bearing material, including electronic scrap, remain in an unresolved category.

The U.S. has yet to become a party to the Basel Convention. That, combined with provisions guaranteeing the priority of national determinations over Basel provisions, leaves U.S. law (and the OECD agreement, where applicable) as controlling exports from America. It appears that the U.S. will not join unless the drafters agree upon some "rational" scheme. In a policy statement three years ago, the U.S. government said it felt that Basel should make it clear that the Convention did not cover "commodities and commodity-like materials." This would include most secondary market precious metals. However, in at least one instance, the U.S. government notified China that materials it was receiving violated Basel though the export did not violate U.S. law. These materials were, in turn, rejected by China. Thus, it seems that the U.S. will try in some fashion to prevent violations of the main thrust of Basel's provisions though it is not a party.

Basel Convention questions remain. One is a liability provision that has the potential to be a sort of international "Superfund." Even if they resolve all other Basel questions, the liability provision, if not drafted carefully, could greatly hamper international trade since no company could afford to take on that scope of liability.

Other factors should also be kept in mind. One is that the relatively sensible

OECD agreement controls the bulk of secondary market precious metals trade. Another is that the ban is on export, not import, so it does not govern imports from non-OECD countries into OECD countries. Finally, in dealing with non-OECD countries, companies must be careful since penalties can be severe (one country allows life imprisonment, a step back from the original proposal-- the death penalty).

> B.   Organization for Economic Cooperation & Development (OECD)

After the signing of the Basel Convention in 1989, but before its ratification, the nations within the OECD began drawing up their own agreement to govern the transfrontier movement of wastes destined for recovery operations. The IPMI participated actively in those deliberations. Under the resultant agreement, the industry has conducted secondary market precious metals trade within the OECD with a minimum of problems, or burdens.

While the OECD agreement was drafted before Basel became binding, it was conceived as a qualifying agreement under Basel Article 11 that permits bilateral, multilateral and regional agreements between nations covering the transboundary movements of hazardous wastes, and other wastes. Whether it is, or is not qualifying, is as yet unresolved.

The OECD agreement established a three-tier system for categorizing wastes:

- Green List: These items move solely under commercial controls. Secondary precious metals in non-dispersible form are on the Green List. They specifically include electronic scrap and spent precious metal-bearing catalysts. Recently, the OECD turned back an effort to remove electronic scrap and spent catalysts from the Green List.

- Amber List
    - First level: This Amber List includes materials in dispersible form, requiring various consent procedures, including pre-approved sites.

- Second level: These Amber List items are based on the constituents that exhibit hazardous characteristics. This control system requires written consent before any transboundary movement can begin, together with all of the other requirements of Amber List materials.

For years, the industry has expected that the U.S. EPA would issue specific regulations regarding the shipment of materials under the OECD agreement. That has never happened, however, and U.S. law that was in effect before the OECD agreement still controls shipments. For example, many industry experts consider secondary precious metals as excluded from certain provisions of RCRA. The EPA is well aware of this position and has not challenged it. Thus, Japan has occasionally sought such a determination from the EPA *before* allowing export under the OECD agreement. Confusion resulted when the EPA, in line with its policy, declined to make such a declaration. In most other instances, Japan has accepted the industry position. Generally, the EPA has been very helpful in facilitating shipments under the OECD agreement and has stated that if U.S. law requires no reporting, it requires no unnecessary filings.

  C. CERCLA Concepts Internationally

    1. Survey of Countries

Many countries incorporate aspects of CERCLA in their property cleanup laws.[133] For example, while CERCLA applies liability to hazardous substances, a few countries limit liability to the narrower category of hazardous wastes (e.g., Argentina).

Most countries seek reimbursement or up-front payment of response costs from responsible parties. Some countries (e.g., Austria), provide government funds to private parties who participate in such responses. Where governments supply funding, monies come from general revenues (e.g., Denmark, Germany, the Netherlands, and Sweden), from taxes/fees on hazardous waste (e.g., Austria), and from water use fees (e.g., Germany).

---

[133] Adapted from: Patterson, "Superfund Liability Abroad," IPMI Environmental Workshop (January 19-21, 1994, Arlington Virginia).

As to liability, while most countries hold present owners/operators responsible, some restrict liability only to that group (e.g., Japan). Many countries have followed CERCLA and impose a strict liability/no-fault approach (e.g., Argentina, Brazil, Germany, and Japan). Similarly, many countries follow CERCLA's joint and several liability scheme (e.g., Austria, Denmark, Germany, and the Netherlands). Most countries, however, depart from CERCLA and do not use retroactive liability. Instead, they prefer to use public funds when the present owners/operators have not contributed to the contamination (e.g., Denmark). Finally, many countries impose liability for actual environmental damage, as opposed to CERCLA's much broader mere "release" trigger.

2.   British Environmental Act of 1995

Great Britain's sweeping Environmental Act of 1995 ("British Act"), provides a unique cross-Atlantic comparison to CERCLA, fifteen years after enactment of the American law. Environmental protection in Britain dates from at least the turn of the century. The British Act, which consolidates much of the prior legislation, is self-described as:

> An Act to provide for the establishment of . . . the Environment Agency . . . to make provision with respect to contaminated land and abandoned mines; to make further provision in relation to National Parks; to make further provision for the control of pollution, the conservation of natural resources and the conservation or enhancement of the environment . . . .[134]

The British Act establishes a catch-all Environment Agency and transfers to it the functions of a variety of existing agencies,[135] for example:

---

[134] British Environmental Act, 1995 Chapter 25, preamble (19th July 1995).

[135] *E.g.*, National Rivers Authority, Waste Regulation Authorities (under the Control of Pollution (Amendment) Act 1989 and the Environmental Pollution Act 1990), Chief Inspector for England and Wales of the Radioactive Substances Act 1993, the Alkali, &c, Works Regulation Act 1906, and Health and Safety at Work etc. Act 1974.

The Agency's pollution control powers shall be exercisable
for the purpose of preventing or minimizing, or remedying
or mitigating the effects of, pollution of the environment.[136]

Importantly, the new Environment Agency ("Agency") must always apply a
cost-benefit analysis to its regulatory activities:

Each new Agency: . . .   shall, unless and to the extent
that it is unreasonable for it to do so in view of the nature
or purpose of the power or in the circumstances of the
particular case, take into account the likely costs and
benefits of the exercise or non-exercise of the power or its
exercise in the manner in question.[137]

By forcing the regulators to consider economic realities, Parliament has
created a powerful pro-business framework for its umbrella environmental
law and new implementing agency.[138]   This type of mandatory cost-benefit
approach may result in *de facto* ceilings for certain Agency-required actions.
For example, the Agency may never direct groundwater cleanups where the
costs will exceed a certain amount or direct equipment upgrades where the
costs will exceed the depreciated value of the machinery.

Before the Agency can require *remediation* of a contaminated property, it
must first designate *contaminated land* as a *special site* and then issue a
remediation notice to all *appropriate persons*. The British Act defines
"remediation" as including:

- Site investigation, or "assessing the condition of (i) the
  contaminated land in question; (ii) any controlled waters

---

[136]   British Act at § 5(1), emphasis added.

[137]   Id. at § 39, emphasis added.

[138]   The original United States Endangered Species Act contained no cost-
benefit elements. After a huge Tennessee Valley Authority watershed project
was completely shut down due to the potential impact on the now infamous
"snail-darter" fish, Congress amended the legislation and include cost-benefit
analysis.

affected by that land; or (iii) any land adjoining or adjacent to that land."[139]

- Removal actions, or "preventing or minimizing, or remedying or mitigating the effects of, any significant harm."[140]
- Remedial actions, or "restoring the land or waters to their former state."[141]
- Post cleanup monitoring, or "making of subsequent inspections from time to time for the purpose of keeping under review the condition of the land or waters."[142]

The new British statutory standard is cleanup to a parcel's "former state."[143] While the debate rages on the U.S. side of the Atlantic as to how-clean-is-clean, the British have adopted unique language susceptible to two very different interpretations. On the one hand, if one could prove the "former state" of a property was part of an old regional problem (e.g., a groundwater plume), then the statute requires little if any additional remediation. On the other hand, if the Agency successfully showed that a "former state" existed before any industrial development, then a "pristine" cleanup might be necessary.

The British Act sets forth a standard of "significant possibility" of harm as the trigger for administrative action, which is less stringent than many American laws that provide for agency action where there is a mere "threat" of adverse impact:

> "Contaminated land" is any land which appears to the local
> authority . . . to be in such a condition, by reason of

---

[139] British Act at §78A(7)(a). The primary American equivalent is the site investigation requirements of the N.C.P. implementing CERCLA. 40 C.F.R. § 300.430.

[140] British Act at §78A(7)(b)(i). The primary American equivalent is the removal elements of the N.C.P. at 40 C.F.R. § 300.415.

[141] British Act at §78A(7)(b)(ii). The primary American equivalent is the remedial action aspects of the N.C.P. at 40 C.F.R. § 300.430(c)-300.435.

[142] British Act at §78A(7)(c). The primary American equivalent is the operation and maintenance portions of the N.C.P. at 40 C.F.R. § 300.435(f).

[143] British Act at §78A(7)(b)(ii).

substances in, on or under the land that: (a) significant harm is being caused or there is a <u>significant possibility</u> of such harm being caused; or (b) pollution of controlled waters is being, or is likely to be, caused.[144]

The designation of a parcel as a "special site" is the key threshold for giving the Agency jurisdiction. While the statutory definition of this key term is lacking,[145] the British Act does use an extremely practical case-by-case approach:

> [The Agency may] make different provisions for different cases or circumstances or different areas or localities and may, in particular describe land [as a special site] by reference to the area or locality in which it is situated.[146]

Once the Agency has made the "special site" designation, it can then issue the "remediation notice" which specifies "what that person is to do by way of remediation and the periods in which he is required to do each of the things so specified."[147] The recipient of the remediation notice has 21 days to appeal such to the magistrate's court or the Secretary of State (who can quash or approve the notice, with or without modification).[148] Failure to comply with the notice can result in fines or being subjected to the full range of powers of the High Court (presumably contempt and even incarceration).[149]

In a close parallel to the dreaded American CERCLA § 106 order,[150] which the EPA issues to responsible parties who are not cooperating, the British

---

[144] <u>Id</u>. at §78A(2), emphasis added.

[145] "A 'special site' is any contaminated land" which still retains its designation as such under the British Act. <u>Id</u>. at §78A(3).

[146] <u>Id</u>. at § 78C(8-9).

[147] <u>Id</u>. at §78E(1).

[148] <u>Id</u>. at §78L(2).

[149] <u>Id</u>. at §78M.

[150] 42 U.S.C. §9606.

remediation notices can require very specific acts:

> Different remediation notices requiring the doing of
> different things by way of remediation may be served on
> different persons in consequence of the presence of different
> substances in, on or under any land or waters.[151]

This phraseology prompts the question as to whether the issuing of different notices can only be based upon "the presences of different substances," or whether the Agency can also segregate such notices based upon other criteria (e.g., volumetric contributions).

Finally with respect to such remediation notices, Parliament authorized an up-front agency determination of the liability of the parties:

> Where two or more persons are *appropriate persons* in
> relation to any particular thing which is to be done by way
> of remediation, the remediation notice served on each of
> them shall state the proportion, determined under [the
> British Act], of the cost of doing that thing which each of
> them respectively is liable to bear.[152]

Given this dramatic all-encompassing liability allocation power, it is important to understand the basis by which the Agency designates "appropriate persons." The British Act sets up two basic categories. The first is for those parties where there is a causal link between the person and the contaminant release (i.e., where there is an element of fault):

> [A]ny person, or any of the persons, who caused or
> knowingly permitted the substances, or any of the
> substances, by reason of which the contaminated land in
> question is such land to be in, or under that land is an
> appropriate person.[153]

---

[151] British Act at §78E(2).

[152] Id. at §78E(3), emphasis added.

[153] Id. at §78F(2), emphasis added.

52

These fault-based appropriate persons are liable for remediation related to their actions on the contaminated land where the release originated.[154] They are also liable for actions on any lands where it appears, to the enforcing authority,[155] that such substances have migrated.[156] The British Act has expressly made fault-based appropriate persons liable for breakdown daughter-products of the substances they released.[157]

The second category of appropriate persons, which comes into play only after a reasonable inquiry fails to produce any fault-based appropriate persons, includes current owners or occupiers of contaminated land they do not link to the release.[158] These owner/occupier appropriate persons are strictly liable, in the same regardless-of-fault fashion as under key U.S. environmental laws,[159] for remediation of the contaminated land that they presently own or occupy.

If the Agency or other enforcing authority deems it necessary to undertake remediation on its own, Parliament gave them ample authority to do so[160] and to recover associated costs from the appropriate persons.[161] Where there is

---

[154] Id. at §78F(3) (liable "in relation to things which are to be done by way of remediation which are to any extent referable to substances which he caused or knowingly permitted to be present in, on or under the contaminated land in question.").

[155] Id. at §78K(7) ("'appear' means appear to the enforcing authority ....").

[156] Id. at §78K(1-5).

[157] Id. at §78K(9).

[158] Id. at §78K(4-5) ("If no person has, after reasonable inquiry, been found who is by virtue of [the fault-based provisions] an appropriate person ... the owner or occupier for the time being of the contaminated land in question is an appropriate person.").

[159] *E.g.,* CERCLA (42 U.S.C. §9600, *et. seq.*); RCRA (42 U.S.C. §6971, *et. seq.*).

[160] British Act at §78N.

[161] Id. at §78P(1).

more than one appropriate person, the government cost recovery is to be in the proportions as determined under the legislation and accompanying Agency-promulgated guidelines.[162]

While many details and practicalities of carrying out the British Act await Agency guidance and court interpretation, the new British law provides a comprehensive scheme for dealing with contaminated land. Since Britain's environmental contamination problems date hundreds of years to the beginning of the industrial revolution, only time will tell how the Environmental Act of 1995 will accomplish its goals.

---

[162] Id.

CHAPTER 6
STATE LAW CONCEPTS

Many states have extensive or unique environmental statutes that may affect industry and precious metals businesses. More frequently than in years past, the federal government is looking to states for ideas on practical and effective regulations. This chapter highlights several state approaches, new and old, which warrant evaluation.

A.   California

A complete review of state laws is beyond the scope of this Handbook. California is thus the focus for several reasons. First, California continues to set trends in environmental regulation. Several factors suggest this leadership role will continue: population (one out of every ten Americans, about 30 million out of 300 million, now live in the "Golden State"), economic power (a state that boasts the world's seventh largest economy), and environmentalism (e.g., the birthplace of groups like the Sierra Club and Surfrider Foundation). Second, California is increasingly adopting risk-based corrective actions. This form of a paradigm shift is essential to the Brownfields movement nationwide (discussed in detail in Chapter 7). Third, the precious metals industry has a significant West Coast presence.

1.   Mine Cleanup Liability Protection

In 1995, California passed a law intended to encourage cleanups of abandoned mines by limiting the liability for pollution caused by cleanup activities.[163] The measure is not applicable to parties that had a prior financial interest in a given mine. However, it does provide an exemption from liability of state, public, and private entities when they carry out approved remediation plans for abandoned mines. Though aimed squarely at the noted Penn Mine in Calaveras County, the measure applies to an estimated 2,500 mines in California that are causing or could cause mine-waste drainage problems.

---

[163]   SB 1108 (Sen. Tim Leslie, R-Roseville).

2. Lawrence Livermore National Laboratory Report

In late 1995, a group of elite scientists from the University of California and the Lawrence Livermore National Laboratory ("LLNL"), produced a massive study of groundwater impacts in California. They focused on contamination caused by petroleum hydrocarbons, particularly the known human carcinogen benzene. The Lawrence Livermore Report's conclusions were striking:

> These dominant effects may include the findings that (1) average benzene concentrations have a high probability of decreasing even if no treatment is attempted, (2) benzene plume lengths rarely extend beyond 250 ft., and (3) over-excavation at sites with shallow groundwater improves the probability of observing a decrease in plume average concentration. [164]

In a bold move, California regulators embraced the Lawrence Livermore Report and announced an intent to allow many gasoline-type contamination sites to naturally degrade, *without an active cleanup*. In other words, California formally adopted Risk-Based Corrective Action ("RBCA"). Specifically, Walt Pettit, Executive Director of the State Water Board, decreed that:

> The LLNL team found that the impacts to the environment from leaking USTs [Underground Storage Tanks] were not as severe as we once thought. The Report also presents a convincing argument that passive bioremediation should be considered as the primary remediation tool in most cases once the fuel leak source has been removed.
>
> . . .
>
> What I propose to you is not in any way inconsistent with existing policies or regulations. However, it does represent a major departure from how we have viewed the threat from leaking USTs. [165]

---

[164] Lawrence Livermore National Laboratory, "California Leaking Underground Fuel Tank (LUFT) Historical Case Analysis," (November 16, 1995).

[165] Walt Pettit, "Lawrence Livermore National Laboratory (LLNL) Report on Leaking Underground Storage Tank (UST) Cleanup," (December 8, 1995), emphasis added.

In turn, each California Regional Water Quality Control Board (RWQCB) is implementing the Lawrence Livermore Report in it own way. The Santa Ana RWQCB (serving Riverside and Orange Counties, just south of Los Angeles) adopted one approach presented by Kenneth Williams, the UST program head:

> Within the Santa Ana Region, a high level of urbanization, a high and increasing dependance on water supply derived from groundwaters[166] and a relatively transmissive aquifer setting combine to create a situation where the groundwater resources are highly valued and susceptible to contamination. . . .
>
> . . . The most noteworthy observation [in rebuttal to the Report] is that a significant percentage of these groundwater cases are older than ten years and yet still exhibit elevated concentrations of benzene. This observation is in contrast to the LLNL report's assertion that petroleum compounds in groundwater rapidly degrade. Staff concurs that degradation by biologic organisms will occur in the subsurface if suitable chemical conditions are present. . . .
>
> With this in mind, staff's recommendation for the definition of "low-risk" cases incorporates two primary criteria. The first criterion is whether the site is situated in an area which does not recharge presently utilized drinking water aquifers. . . .
>
> The second criterion for the definition of "low-risk" cases would identify sites where the levels of contamination are sufficiently low so as to be assumed to be addressed by the passive bioremediation processes discussed in the LLNL report. Such sites would not appear to pose a threat to the water resources in the Region. Specifically, staff recommends that the following thresholds be used to define such sites [where MCL's represent existing state-wide

---

[166] More than 50% of the drinking water in Orange County (population over 2 million) comes from groundwater beneath the region.

Maximum Contaminant Levels in drinking water]:

Constituent	MCL's	"Low-risk" threshold
Benzene	1 ppb	250 ppb [250 times higher]
Toluene	150 ppb	300 ppb [2 times higher]
Ethyl benzene	680 ppb	680 ppb [same]
Xylene	1750 ppb	1750 ppb [same]

For cases where the impacts to the underlying groundwaters do not currently exceed these levels, groundwater monitoring would provide the confirmation that the contaminant concentrations are diminishing.[167]

California is not alone in embracing such RBCA approaches. A recent national survey,[168] on regulatory attitudes toward natural attenuation, places the states into the following six categories:

- Do not allow natural attenuation.[169]
- No policy on natural attenuation, but would consider allowing.[170]
- Informal policies allowing natural attenuation.[171]
- Implicit policies allowing natural attenuation.[172]

---

[167] Ken Williams, "Direction of the Underground Tank Program," California Regional Water Quality Control Board, Santa Ana Region (Jan. 26, 1996).

[168] The survey results are adapted from: "Many States Consider Passive Remediation," Geraghty & Miller's The Groundwater Newsletter, p. 2 (February 15, 1996)

[169] Six state agency departments will not consider natural attenuation as a stand-alone remedial option because of heavy reliance on groundwater.

[170] The majority of states fall into this category. While they have no guidelines, they would consider such on a case-by-case basis if proposed responsibly.

[171] Site assessment and monitoring are crucial to states having informal guidelines.

[172] E.g., the "Emergency Standard Guide for Risk-Based Corrective Action Applied at Petroleum Sites," ASTM report ES38-94, is being formally used in at least two states.

- Written policy allowing natural attenuation.[173]
- Expecting policy changes on natural attenuation.[174]

In limited situations, natural attenuation will be *more* expensive because the cost of monitoring for extended periods may exceed active removal actions. The natural attenuation option may be most attractive for large industrial concerns on established properties, where regulators "stay off their backs" and allow infrequent testing over the years.

3.   Single Agency Designation ("Certificate of Completion")

The innovative Single Agency Designation law,[175] allows the California Environmental Protection Agency (Cal-EPA) to designate a single state or local agency to oversee site investigation and cleanup. The state then grants the administering agency sole jurisdiction over all activities necessary for the response action. This approach reduces the costs and confusion associated with overlapping and sometimes conflicting instructions from competing agencies.

The law also provides that once a cleanup is done to the satisfaction of the appointed lead agency, Cal-EPA will issue a "Certificate of Completion." This Certificate acknowledges that the cleanup meets all relevant state and local requirements. Unless new information later shows fraud or other extraordinary circumstance, no state or local agency may take further enforcement action on a certified site. This Certificate should greatly ease transactions related to impacted properties (e.g., financing, sales, leases, etc.). A Certificate should be sought or required to achieve maximum closure on formerly-contaminated properties, beyond what is otherwise available through the typical agency "no further action" letter.

---

[173]   Only New Jersey and North Carolina have specific written policies concerning natural attenuation as a stand-alone remedial option.

[174]   Several states (including LA, MN, WI, FL, IA, and KY) are expected to make policy changes in 1996.

[175]   California Health and Safety Code §25260 *et. seq.*, "Unified Agency Review of Hazardous Materials Release Sites," effective January 1, 1994.

4.   Nuisance

California courts continue to expand nuisance as a vehicle for recovering a wide range of damages for property contamination. A plaintiff whose property is injured or whose personal enjoyment is lessened by a nuisance may sue under that theory.[176] California's statutory definition of nuisance broadly includes:

> Anything which is injurious to health, or is indecent or offensive to the senses, or an obstruction to the free use of property, so as to interfere with the comfortable enjoyment of life or property ...[177]

In the environmental context, courts recognize California's nuisance law may encompass almost every conceivable type of interference with the enjoyment or use of land.[178] The cases have held that a subsequent purchaser of contaminated land may maintain a nuisance suit against a prior occupier of land.[179] It is immaterial whether the nuisance was created at some past time. For example, the author's law firm recently secured a $1.75 million settlement on behalf of a landowner in a nuisance case for lead contamination occurring between 1903 and 1946.[180] This type of liability has lasting impacts:

> Before Mangini, the way the law worked is that if you were a property owner and you didn't interfere with the rights of other people around your property, the public or adjoining property owners or your tenants or whatever, as long as you behaved in a proper fashion and you disclosed everything that you know to the person who bought from you, you

---

[176] California Code Civ. Proc. § 731.

[177] California Civil Code §3479.

[178] *See* Wilshire Westwood Assoc. v. Atlantic Richfield Co., 20 Cal.App.4th 732, 746(1993).

[179] *E.g.*, Mangini v. Aerojet-General Corp., 230 Cal.App.3d 1125 (1991), Wilshire Westwood, supra., Capogeannis v. Superior Court, 12 Cal.App.4th 668 (1993).

[180] Birtcher Riverside Marketplace Partners v. Union Pacific Railroad, No. CV-93-997 (1993-1996).

were off the hook. I mean, that was it. You had done your
duty to society and you could go on with your life and not
have to worry about 20 or 30 years down the road
somebody suing you for something you did while you
owned that property in the past.[181]

Nuisance cases generally apply general tort measure of damages,
compensation for all the detriment proximately caused by the defendant (even
if not foreseeable).[182] Courts have also used flexibility in equity to craft
appropriate remedies for nuisance:

Living as we do in a world of change, equitable remedies
have necessarily and steadily been <u>expanded to meet
increasing complexities of such changing times</u>, and no
inflexible rule has been permitted to circumscribe the power
of equity to do justice. As has been well said, equity has
contrived remedies so that they shall correspond both to the
primary right of the injured party, and to the wrong by
which the right has been violated, and has always <u>preserved
the elements of flexibility and expansiveness</u>, so that new
ones may be invented and old ones modified, in order to
meet the requirement of every case, and to satisfy the needs
of a progressive social condition, in which new primary
rights and duties are constantly arising.[183]

Some courts have taken extreme views on fashioning remedies. For
example, in the <u>Bixby Ranch</u> case,[184] the court required the defendants to pay
plaintiffs nearly $1 million for the permanent <u>post</u>-cleanup "stigma" at the

---

[181] "Private Party Cost Recovery Under CERCLA and RCRA and the
Common Law," <u>Environmental Law News</u>, Vol. 4, No. 4, p. 16 (Winter
1995-1996).

[182] *See, e.g.*, <u>Coats v. Atchison T. & S.F. Ry.</u>, 1 Cal.App. 441 (1905).

[183] <u>Cassinos v. Union Oil Co.</u>, 14 Cal.App.4th 1770,1786-87 (2nd Dist.
1993) (citations omitted) emphasis added.

[184] <u>Bixby Ranch Co. v. Spectrol Technologies</u>, Los Angeles County
Superior Court #052566 (1994).

property. The plaintiffs in <u>Bixby Ranch</u> supported their stigma claim in part by alleging that a future buyer or tenant would discount the value of the property. They deemed such discounts necessary to compensate for expensive pre-purchase due diligence and for the possibility of future additional government regulations.

5. Trespass

A continuing trespass theory may be applied in situations where contaminants have been left by a prior property owner or operator.[185] California courts recognize both private and public nuisance as 'tortious conduct' which will support a claim for trespass.[186]

B. Pennsylvania

Pennsylvania was a pioneer in environmental regulation. For example, in 1682, the state passed a law protecting forest lands from fire. In 1721, Pennsylvania established seasonal limits on hunting. This colonial tradition continued after American Independence. In 1866, the state created the Fish Commission, followed in 1895 by the Game Commission.[187] The nation's first effort to protect water supplies against pollution occurred with the 1905 passage of the Pennsylvania Purity of Waters Act.[188] The Clean Streams Law of 1937 and the Air Pollution Control Act of 1960 were similar efforts to preserve and protect Pennsylvania's environment.[189]

---

[185] *E.g.,* <u>KFC Western, Inc. v. Meghrig</u>, 23 Cal.App.4th 1167, 1181 (1993).

[186] <u>Id</u>. at 1182.

[187] Pennsylvania Business Roundtable, <u>Environmental Issues Task Force Report</u> 83 (1986).

[188] *See* Act of April 22, 1905, P.L. 260, No. 182 (codified as amended at 35 P.S. §§711-716, repealed May 1, 1984, P.L. 206, No. 43, §18, replaced by PA. STAT. ANN., tit. 35, §§721.1-21.17 (Pardon 1993)).

[189] The Clean Streams Law, act of June 22, 1937, P.L. 1987, No. 394 (codified at PA. STAT. ANN. tit. 35, §§691.1-691.1001 (Pardon 1993)); Air Pollution Control act of Jan. 8, 1960, P.L. (1959) 2119, §1 (codified at PA. STAT. ANN. tit. 35 §§4001-4106 (Pardon 1993)).

Pennsylvania has a progressive clean air program that has gained nationwide recognition.[190] Under the federal Clean Air Act, states identify and designate all areas that do not satisfy the national standards for any contaminant ("non-attainment areas"). The Pennsylvania Department of Environmental Resources (DER) has also adopted an emission offset policy. This scheme ensures that the air within a non-attainment region does not get worse because of new sources or modifications of existing sources and that they make progress toward achieving the national standards. The offset policy requires most new sources and modifications of existing sources to obtain emission reductions (offsets) to alleviate the ambient impact of the new source. They may create the offsets internally (within the same facility or source) or externally (at a different facility). The offset ratios that the DER enforces, all greater than one to one, will improve air quality in a non-attainment area during operation of a new source.

Source owners or operators may "bank" emission offsets with DER. This market-based aspect of the program benefits owners and operators who achieve emission reductions through curtailment or shutdown of their operations, or through improved emission control or operating techniques. Such parties may either bank the offset amount for future use or transfer, or with DER's approval, sell the offsets to other facilities. However, the DER regulations and the Pennsylvania State Implementation Plan impose detailed requirements, including applying to DER and time limitations. Further, applicants may not use emission reductions banked before January 1991 for emission offsets. The state has established a registry system for emission reduction credits from existing sources to new or modified sources.

    C.   New Jersey

New Jersey's older Environmental Cleanup Responsibility Act (ECRA)[191] requires investigation and cleanup before transfers or closure of certain

---

[190] Adapted from: Mattioni, <u>Pennsylvania Environmental Law Handbook</u>, Government Institutes, Inc., p. 43-45 (1994).

[191] N.J. Rev. Stat. §§ 13:1 *et. seq.*

industrial facilities.[192]   One commentator summarized:[193]

- ECRA moved disclosure to the new plane of an obligation to investigate for the presence of contamination before certain transactions. New Jersey thus established a mechanism for the detection of contaminated properties that is a random proposition in other states.

- New Jersey moves government to an unprecedented degree in these property transfers. Until the state has approved the investigation, and made provisions for remedial activities, the transfer cannot occur. This feature has hopelessly bogged down the state bureaucracy.

- ECRA is the most comprehensive statute of its kind. While no state has been bold enough to copy ECRA precisely, recognizing its practical problems, many states are studying it.[194]

ECRA is triggered by the "closing, terminating, or transferring of operations."[195]   Within five days of an agreement to transfer ownership, the parties must give notice to the state, and within 45 days submit an environmental sampling plan.[196]   For "clean" sites, after the state's inspection, it files a negative declaration attesting to no discharge of hazardous substances or wastes, or that the parties remediated any problems.[197]   If an investigation reveals the site is contaminated, the parties

---

[192]   Under ECRA, industrial establishments are those which "involve the generation, manufacture, refining, transportation, treatment, storage, handling, or disposal of hazardous substances or wastes [including petroleum products] on-site, above or below ground." Id. at §§ 13:1K-8(d),(f) and -9.

[193]   Adapted from: Moskowitz, Environmental Liability and Real Property Transactions: Law and Practice, (1989 & 1991).

[194]   Id. at § 12.

[195]   N.J. Rev. Stat. § 13:1K-8(b). This definition includes virtually all changes in ownership (e.g., mergers and bankruptcy filings). Id.

[196]   N.J. Admin. Code §§ 7:26B-5.

[197]   Id.

must submit a cleanup plan.[198] Where there is a failure to follow ECRA, the buyer or the state may void the transaction (providing damages in the private party-voiding situation).[199]

Cleanup costs incurred under ECRA have been judicially construed as "damages" such that an insurer had indemnity obligations.[200] Crest-Foam Corp. operated a foam manufacturing plant from 1965 to 1986 when it sold all outstanding stock. The transfer plan triggered ECRA and Crest-Foam notified the state Department of Environmental Protection (NJDEP) and conducted an environmental investigation. After they found soil and groundwater contamination, Crest-Foam entered an administrative consent order with the NJDEP.

New Jersey also now has economic incentives for Brownfields redevelopment since Governor Christine Todd-Whitman's signing of the 1996 Environmental Opportunity Zone Act.[201] Contaminated sites may be eligible for a 10-year property tax exemption if the remediation complies with state standards. Municipalities may also designate properties as environmental opportunity zones eligible for cleanup loans and tax exemptions. The EOZ statute has the following preface:

> The Legislature finds that there are numerous properties that are underutilized or that have been abandoned and that are not being utilized for any commercial use because of contamination that exists at those properties; that abandoned contaminated properties harm society by causing a burden on municipal services while failing to contribute to the funding of those services; that a disproportionate percentage of these properties are located in older urban municipalities given the fact that these municipalities were once the center

---

[198] Id.

[199] Id. at § B-9.1

[200] Crest-Foam Corp. v. Hartford Accident & Indemnity Co., No. L-1068-93, N.H. Super. Ct. (January 24, 1996).

[201] "Brownfields Time has Come," Geraghty & Miller's The Groundwater Newsletter, p. 5 (Jan. 31, 1996).

for industrial production; that revitalization of these properties will not only bring taxes to the municipality and other local governments, but will result in job creation and foster urban redevelopment . . . .[202]

This statute may reflect New Jersey's shift from an overenthusiastic regulator to an economic promoter of "Brownfields" site cleanups.

---

[202] New Jersey P.L. 1996, Chapter 413 (approved January 10, 1996).

CHAPTER 7
CONTAMINATED PROPERTIES

A.   Brownfields Redevelopment

Over the last decade, red-tape and legal battles bogged down the investigation and cleanup of contaminated properties. In response, federal and local governments moved to ease the return of contaminated urban properties to productive use. The resulting "Brownfields" redevelopment typically involves an assignment of risk or relief from environmental liability, streamlining of governmental action, and coordinating cleanup with development activities.

Participants in this emerging market include property owners or holders of security interests in contaminated properties.[203] Major players include mining, oil and gas, refining, utilities, manufacturing, finance, insurance, and fund management participants (e.g., pensions). Sellers frequently ask the following questions: Is there a market for our property? What is it worth? How extensive is our residual liability? What are the tax and financial reporting consequences? What are the overall implications for shareholder value?

Purchasers include real estate developers, equity investors, lenders, remedial contractors, insurers, indemnitors, and users. This group typically asks questions such as: What is the highest and best use of the property? What cleanup standards apply? How can we limit liability? What types of properties should we be looking at and how can we find them? What are the financing options? What types of returns can we expect?

The following are examples of this important trend:[204]

---

[203] Adapted from: "Contaminated Property Transactions," Coopers & Lybrand (1996).

[204] "Brownfields' Time has Come," Geraghty & Miller's The Groundwater Newsletter, p. 5 (Jan. 31, 1996).

- A Congressional study notes that potential U.S. Brownfields site estimates range from tens of thousands to nearly 450,000. New York City has noted that many of the 4,000 acres of vacant property in the city are Brownfields candidates resulting from past industrial activity. Chicago determined that its metropolitan area has more than 2,000 potential Brownfields properties.

- In late 1995, the federal Brownfields Economic Redevelopment Initiative selected an additional 11 new pilot projects from 130 municipal applications. As of early 1996, 40 of the planned 50 projects in the program have been selected.

- On January 4, 1996, Rep. William Coyne (D-PA) introduced a new Brownfields Redevelopment Act (H.R. 2846) which would offer a 50% federal tax credit to "innocent" owners toward remediation expenses on EPA or state-approved cleanups. Eligible sites must have been out of use for at least a year, be unlikely redevelopment candidates, be likely to create jobs, expand a city's tax base, and redevelop quickly.

- On January 25, 1996, the EPA announced that they will delete an additional 3,300 sites from the national inventory of potential Superfund sites. This means more than 27,000 sites (two-thirds of the inventory) are no longer of federal interest. Until the EPA began removing sites in 1995 from the previous list of 38,000, developers and lenders avoid them.

About 25 states have adopted laws or rules to reduce the threat of liability and adjust treatment standards on contaminated urban sites. For example, Minnesota has cut red tape to reduce average Brownfields regulatory delays and Massachusetts enacted private-manager legislation authorizing private experts to supervise certain site cleanups.

B.   Facility Purchases/Acquisitions

While a hazardous waste investigation is vital in real property purchases, it can be a deal breaker. Sophisticated buyers carefully evaluate the risk of contamination. To start the process, attached as Appendix "E" is a *Preliminary Environmental Audit Form.*

1.   Attorney Confidentiality

Understandably, sellers and buyers wish to keep many aspects of contaminated property transactions private. One key way to do so is to protect information under the attorney confidentiality umbrella.   The "attorney-client privilege" protects confidential communications between a client and an attorney to encourage "full and frank disclosure by the client to his or her attorney."[205] Similarly, the "work product doctrine" protects litigation materials that reveal an attorney's strategies and evaluations.[206] The doctrine preserves the privacy of attorneys' thoughts and prevents opposing parties "borrowing the wits of their adversaries."[207]

Businesses should thus try to channel environmental matters through their counsel. For example, the attorneys should hire consultants to best shield the consultant's work and opinions. One handy tool to accomplish this is by entering into a *Master Consulting Agreement*, attached as Appendix "F." In this fashion, a company maximizes its ability to resist disclosure to third parties in the future.

2.   Description of Process

The process of evaluating properties for environmental concerns has evolved over the last decade.   As summarized by the Environmental Bankers Association:

> The first level of environmental site assessment is the Phase I Environmental Site Assessment (Phase I ESA). The scope may be one of several developed by industry associations or one developed by your bank [and/or to suit the particular

---

[205] Clarke v. American Commerce Nat'l Bank, 974 F.2d 127, 129 (9th Cir., 1992).

[206] Hickman v. Taylor, 329 U.S. 495 (1947); F.R.C.P. 26(b)(3).

[207] Hickman, supra.; Holmgren v. State Farm, 976 F.2d 573 (9th Cir., 1992).

needs of the purchaser].[208] A Phase I ESA is an assessment
of potential on-site contamination or liability that may result
from historical and current property uses. A Phase I ESA
covers review of government records about environmental
matters, interviews with government officials and property
owners, a site visit and preparation of a written report based
on the work. In some cases, an abbreviated version of a
Phase I ESA, referred to as a Transaction Screen Process
Environmental Site Assessment,[209] may be used.

When the first level of investigation indicates a potential
environmental impact to groundwater, soil, or air, then
further work is required (sometimes called a Phase II for
which there now is no precise standard, because
requirements for each site could differ). This further
investigation could include laboratory analysis of soil,
water, air or other material samples taken from the site by
environmental professionals according to strict sampling
protocols and quality control methods. If necessary, more
than one round of sampling analysis may be conducted,
especially to measure the extent of soil and/or groundwater
contaminant, and to prepare estimates for any cleanup that
may be required by environmental laws and regulations.[210]

3.   Managing Transactional Risks

The buyer of contaminated property may attempt to limit liability by
transferring the property into a separate corporation or other protective

---

[208] The most commonly adopted standard for a Phase I ESA is:
American Society for Testing and Materials (ASTM), "Standard Practice for
Environmental Site Assessments: Phase I environmental Site Assessment
Process," ASTM Designation: E 1527-94 (current edition approved April 15,
1994).

[209] The most commonly adopted standard for a Transaction Screen is:
ASTM, "Standard Practice for Environmental Site Assessments: Transaction
Screen Process," ASTM Designation: E 1528-93 (current edition approved
March 15, 1993).

[210] Environmental Bankers Association, "Your Bank, Your Business and
The Environment, " p. 7 (November, 1994).

business form.[211] The likelihood of success in limiting liability in this fashion may depend on the individual or corporate owner's level of control over, and capitalization of, the new entity.

Parties may also seek to limit liability by including a recitation of known contamination or other conditions affecting the site in the property conveyance. Indemnifications that cover one or more site conditions may accompany such a recitation. These statements may stand alone and serve as a reference point for determining questions about whether a specific contamination problem was disclosed, or whether it resulted from the activities of the seller or buyer after the purchase. To prepare a thorough recitation, detailed knowledge of the property operations and subsurface conditions is necessary.

The seller may be asked to warrant that the site is clean and provide representations and disclosures regarding environmental compliance of the facility. Failure to disclose environmental problems or liabilities can constitute fraud. Conversely, the seller may seek to convey the property "as is" to transfer all potential liability for environmental matters to the buyer.

An escrow account can be established for future investigation and cleanup costs. Also, obtaining a bond for the environmental response costs may be possible. A buyer could also use such a bond arrangement for the amount of the loan. Finally, a potential buyer may lease the property, instead of an outright purchase. While this maneuver will not protect the buyer against liability as an operator, it may preclude "owner" liability.

C.   Environmental Consultants

1.   The Selection Process

"Environmental consultant" is an umbrella phrase that encompasses the following professionals: environmental engineers, geologists, hydro-geologists, chemists, and environmental economists. Capabilities and experience vary greatly among environmental consulting firms. Many firms market that they "do just about everything." While this may be technically

---

[211] Adapted from: Cooke, The Law of Hazardous Waste, supra. (1995).

correct (e.g., they did once do a few borings at the site that had PCB's), in-depth specific and local experience is paramount.

The size of environmental firms must fit the size of the problem. For example, larger firms, who can pull from talent and offer services nationally and internationally, may be the front runners on large projects. Yet, where the project is of a lesser scale, or has more commonly encountered problems, local specialty firms may be perfect.

As an example of a matrix that may help in the consultant selection process, a *Phase I Consultant Selection Checklist* is attached as Appendix "G."

2. Where Cleanup Dollars Really Go

In trying to stretch cash as far as possible, it is extremely helpful to know where cleanup dollars really go. The analysis below excludes consideration of attorneys' fees (i.e., presumes a voluntary cleanup). While projects vary widely, the following example focuses on the most common scenario: soil and groundwater contamination. These response actions typically involve five phases:

- Investigation involves subsurface property testing and corresponding laboratory work, with written reports of results and recommendations for further action.
- Design is the creation of specifications and design of the remediation system.
- Construction involves the purchase and assembly of the remediation system.
- Operation and maintenance ("O&M") are the processes of running the remediation system over the life of the cleanup.
- Closure is the process of verifying that the site has reached a certain cleanup level and negotiating with the responsible agency for sign-off.

While site response actions will obviously vary, the following survey indicates the relative proportions among the five phases:[212]

- Investigation   20%
- Design   6-10%

---

[212] Jeff Gwinn, Orion Environmental, Long Beach, California (310/433-7971).

- Construction   13-21%
- O&M   36-48%
- Closure   12-13%

The investigation phase comprises only about 20% of the total cleanup costs. This factor must be kept in mind when discussing financial resources and budgeting. If $30,000 has already been spent for an investigation, and technical staff estimates and additional $30,000 in investigation (thus $60,000 total), the cleanup total may reach $300,000. Site conditions may skew the percentages dramatically. For instance, if the soils matrix were to be clay, rather than coarse-grain (e.g., sand/gravel), the percentage of O&M costs would increase significantly given the increased difficulty in leaching out contaminants.

3. Developing a Short List

It is preferable to develop a short list of three to five firms who appear to meet general selection criteria (e.g., location and applicable experience). A first good source for consultant recommendations is attorneys who do a sufficient volume of environmental work. A second source is repeat clients in high risk businesses (e.g., oil companies, auto service chains, heavy industry, etc.). Large corporations are narrowing the number of firms they use. As a result, they have often performed detailed cost and quality evaluations. Finally, agencies may be a source of information on qualified firms. However, this approach is limited since many agencies feel it improper to make specific recommendations.

4. The Request for Proposal

The Request for Proposal ("RFP") should describe the scope and reason for the work, any existing or anticipated problem areas, and generically identify customers. The RFP should describe the project in detail, referencing prior studies and any areas of suspected contamination. The site description should include the following elements:

- The street address and telephone number.
- A site map with as much detail as practical as to aboveground and subsurface structures, both existing and historic (e.g., machine or processing areas, drum storage, underground storage tanks, clarifiers, or piping).

- The location of any significant neighboring operations.
- Prior environmental investigations, status of agency involvement.

The scope of work section should describe the amount and type of work needed. The first approach to detailing the scope of work is to provide a standardized bid-response form. This approach has lower front end costs since there is limited engineering time. Yet, it produces a broader range of bids because of the inherent flexibility afforded the consultant in choosing approaches (e.g., the size of the monitoring wells). The second approach is to describe, in as much detail as possible, the work to be done and the approach. While this method necessarily involves a higher preparation cost (e.g., an outside consultant or technically qualified attorney preparing the specific scope), it has the advantage of narrowing the range of bids. The preparer, not the bidding consultant, is specifying the methodology.

With respect to bidding requirements, the RFP should list any special requirements that the prospective bidders must meet. Special requirements under this category may include the following items:

- Experience
- References
- Minimum staff qualifications
- Availability
- Insurance

For instance, the author's firm sought consulting services for a municipality. The client had recently shut down several drinking water wells because of solvent contamination. Since they contemplated litigation, many detailed questions in the RFP had a legal-orientation:

- Project Manager: Please attach a *litigation biography* for the proposed local project manager (as opposed to any national talent that they may call upon for specialized support). The focus here is on litigation nuts-and-bolts, rather than project similarity. For example, at least the following information is important:

  - Number of cases on which the individual has served as a litigation support project manager (not merely doing staff work in support of someone else acting as Project Manager).

  - The approximate number of times they have deposed the individual, with approximate time estimates for such (e.g., three depositions less than four hours, two depositions between four and six hours, and three depositions more than six hours).

- The number of days of trial testimony the individual has given, approximating the time on the stand for such days.

- For each of the three above subcategories, indications of the approximate percentage of time in the following three categories: environmental, geotechnical, and other (e.g., depositions: environmental [70%], geotechnical [10%], other [20%]).

- Reference to one attorney who has examined the individual on the stand at trial and/or defended him at deposition.

In response to this approach, one firm completely withdrew (to "not waste everyone's time"). For the consultants who did respond, expertise in litigation and support was clear. The short list proceeded to focused personal interviews and selection of the "winner" based upon the client's real needs.

CHAPTER 8
ENVIRONMENTAL RISK MANAGEMENT

Businesses can ignore, react to, or progressively manage environmental risk. The first is dangerous, the second expensive, and the last is prudent. The following reviews how environmental liabilities may impact companies and outlines several tools for managing the risk.

A.   Scope of Liability

Over the past twenty years, environmental compliance has evolved into a major civil and criminal risk for corporations operating in the U.S. and internationally. Increasingly, the scope of this liability extends to individual shareholders, officers, and directors of a corporation.

1.   The Corporate Veil

As a separate legal entity, a corporation is responsible for its own debts.[213] Normally, the shareholders, directors, and officers of the corporation are not legally responsible for corporate liabilities. If the business has losses, the corporation bears them to the extent of its own resources. The stockholders indirectly bear losses in that the value of their stock declines proportionally. This system of protection is the backbone of several hundred years of corporate law (first in England, then in the U.S. and the rest of the world).

In certain cases, courts disregard the corporate entity ("pierce the corporate veil") and hold shareholders personally liable. This typically happens because of the manner that the shareholders deal with the corporation. For example, shareholders may fail to adequately capitalize the corporation or maintain corporate formalities. Courts regard such "piercing" as a drastic remedy and disregard the corporate form only reluctantly. Yet, under

---

[213] These sections include material from: C. Hugh Friedman, California Practice Guide: Corporations (The Rutter Group, 1994); Susan M. Cooke, The Law of Hazardous Waste, supra. (1995). Much of this discussion is applicable to limited liability companies ("LLC's") and limited liability partnerships ("LLP's").

certain environmental statutes (e.g., CERCLA), courts are increasingly willing to hold shareholders and individuals personally liable.

2. Shareholders

In one case,[214] a court found two major shareholders of a corporation personally liable under CERCLA for contamination of a site where they shipped hazardous wastes. The shareholders were the founder/president of the corporation and a vice president/facility supervisor. Both men planned and carried out the corporation's waste disposal practices, had personal knowledge of the company's hazardous substances and wastes, and arranged for transportation of wastes. Because of this *active participation*, the Court found both shareholders personally liable as "owners" or "operators" under Section 107(a) of CERCLA. In doing so, the Court noted that the shareholders had "the capacity to prevent and abate the damage caused by the disposal of hazardous wastes" at the site.[215]

3. Officers and Directors

Using the same analysis, courts have imposed environmental liability on corporate officers and directors personally. Judges give CERCLA's broad definition of "person," a "liberal interpretation that may include both the employee and the corporation."[216]

4. Parent Corporation and Subsidiaries

Courts usually treat a parent corporation and its subsidiaries as separate and distinct legal entities. This is not so where the parent controls the subsidiary and there is such a unity of interest that they do not really function as separate entities. The precise criterion supporting such a determination

---

[214] United States v. Northeastern Pharmaceutical & Chemical Co., Inc., 570 F. Supp. 823 (W.D. Mo. 1984) *affirmed in part, reversed in part*, 810 F.2d 726 (8th cir. 1986), *cert. denied*, 484 U.S. 848, 108 S. Ct. 146 (1987).

[215] *See also*, United States v. Larry Gurley, et al., 43 F.3d. 1188 (8th Cir., 1994), holding that William Gurley, principal shareholder and president of Gurley Refining Co., was liable as an "operator" under CERCLA for site cleanup because he had the authority to determine the company's waste disposal activities and exercised that authority.

[216] Northeastern Pharmaceutical, supra.

varies by jurisdiction. However, courts have pierced the corporate veil and imposed liability on the parent in the following circumstances:

- Intermingling of business transactions, property, employees, accounts, and records of the parent and subsidiary
- Failure to observe the formalities of separate corporate procedures for each corporation
- Inadequate capitalization of the subsidiary
- The enterprises are held out to the public as a single enterprise
- The policies of the subsidiary are directed by the parent

5. Successor Corporations

Courts do not typically find purchasers of a corporation's assets liable for the seller's environmental problems. However, courts will impose such liability where one or more of the following exceptions apply:[217]

- The successor expressly, or otherwise, assumes such liabilities
- Fraudulent use of separate corporate entities to avoid liability
- The purchase constitutes a *de facto* merger or consolidation
- The successor is a mere continuation of the predecessor ("business continuation" theory)

Corporations should thus use extreme skill and caution in acquiring part or all of another company's business. They should also consider the legal effect of such transactions carefully.

B. Risk Avoidance Strategies

1. Risk Management Program

Business can reduce environmental risk through a comprehensive environmental risk management program, including:[218]

---

[217] 15 Fletcher Cyclopedia of the Law of Private Corporations, §7122 (Rev. perm. Ed. 1990).

[218] Adapted from material by Willis Corroon (Nashville, Tennessee).

Risk Identification and Analysis: Identification of risks.
Measurement of loss potential. Estimates of remediation costs.
Quantification of environmental liabilities.

Environmental Loss Control: Review of pollution control design.
Development of environmental policy statements and written
procedures. Employee training and executive briefings on
environmental liability. Processing of environmental claims.

Environmental Contracting Risk Management: Evaluation of
capabilities of consultants and contractors. Review of contracts for
professional consulting or contracting services. Analysis of
contractors' insurance requirements and indemnity agreements.
Review of insurance programs of environmental consultants and
contractors.

Real Estate Transactions, Merger & Acquisition Environmental
Risks: Environmental due diligence. Review specifications for
environmental assessment services. Develop inspection protocols
and report formats. Review of risk assessment reports. Review of
contract documents and indemnity agreements. Environmental
insurance for real estate transfers.

Environmental Insurance: Pollution liability and on-site cleanup
coverages. Financial responsibility for hazardous materials storage.
Closure/post-closure care costs for waste disposal facilities.
Remediation cost overrun and remediation efficacy insurance.
Owner controlled insurance for contaminated sites. Executive
protection from environmental liabilities.

Financial Management of Environmental Costs: Management of the
costs of site remediation. Compliance with environmental laws.
Interface with the financial industry (e.g., direct lenders,
underwriters, brokers).

2.   Attorney Confidentiality Protection for Audits

Many corporations have been slow to conduct internal or third-party audits to
identify and address their pollution problems. One reason is entirely
understandable: the government could force companies to reveal audit
reports with alleged violations and use the reports against them. However,

pursuant to a 1995 EPA policy,[219] businesses may find protection when voluntarily identifying, disclosing, and promptly correcting violations.[220] While the policy stops short of carving out an evidentiary privilege, it does provide four incentives for businesses to "self-police" environmental compliance:

- The EPA will assess no "gravity-based" penalties for those who reveal a violation discovered as part of an audit. A gravity-based penalty is one that is above the amount of economic benefit the business obtained from the violation. The EPA will still insist on recovering that economic benefit as a penalty.

- Where business reports the violation voluntarily although not found as part of a systematic audit, the agency will still reduce gravity-based penalties by 75%.

- The EPA will not recommend criminal enforcement against any business for a violation uncovered as part of an audit, provided the violation does not show: (a) prevalent management philosophy or practice to conceal or condone environmental violations; or (b) high-level corporate officials' or managers' conscious involvement in, or willful blindness to, the violations. The EPA retains the right to recommend criminal sanctions for individual managers even if it lets the company off the hook because of its cooperation.

- The EPA will not request or use an environmental audit report to initiate a civil or criminal investigation nor will it request an audit report as a part of a routine inspection. However, if the agency has independent reason to believe that a violation may have occurred, it may seek audit information to help it identify a violation or to set liability or extent of harm.

---

[219] 60 Federal Register p. 6669 (December 22, 1995), replacing a policy from 1986.

[220] "Federal Audit Privilege Policy Announced," Geraghty & Miller's The Groundwater Newsletter, p. 6 (January 31, 1996); "EPA Finalizes Environmental Audit Proposal," California Environmental Insider, p. 12 (February 15, 1996).

To enjoy any of the incentives, the business must:

- Uncover the violation through an environmental audit or through another form of "systematic" due-diligence
- Identify the violation voluntarily and not through mandatory monitoring or sampling
- Disclose the violation to the EPA within 10 days after discovery
- Discover and disclose the violation without any government or independent prompting (e.g., no whistle-blower reporting)
- Correct the violation within 60 days or the shortest possible period if correction is not possible within that time
- Agree in writing to take steps to prevent recurrence of the violation
- Not have committed the violation (or any closely related violation) within the last three years at the same facility and not had a pattern of similar violations
- Not have seriously harmed or substantially endangered human health or the environment by the violation
- Cooperate with the EPA

Similarly, last year a Federal District Court in California held that the attorney-client privilege protected the findings of a corporate environmental compliance audit.[221] The supervisor of environmental engineering and safety for a defendant prepared an environmental audit before the plaintiff sued. The defendant withheld the audit, claiming attorney-client privilege because the corporation had commissioned the audit to help in-house attorneys evaluating the company's environmental compliance. The court refused to make the defendant hand over the audit because the documents "appear to have been prepared for the purpose of securing an opinion of law."

      3.   Insurance

      a.   CGL Policies Covering Old Releases

Insurance can provide substantial defense and indemnity payments for environmental claims, or none whatsoever, depending upon the policy and nature of the claim. Liability insurance first appeared in the United States in

---

[221] Adapted from: Alpert, "Smart Companies Need to Embrace Auditing," Pollution Engineering, p. 71 (February 1995).

the 1880's.[222] At first, businesses purchased a separate liability policy for each type of risk. As insurers gained experience in evaluating risks, they abandoned the separate policy approach. The new "schedule liability" method permitted buyers to insure several types of risks with one contract. However, since separate terms and conditions governed each type of coverage, the insurance package was complex and confusing. In 1941, the industry developed comprehensive general liability ("CGL") insurance. The CGL policy combined all of the coverages in a single broad insuring agreement. CGL insurance provides coverage for all business liability exposures known to exist at the inception of the policy and all unforeseen hazards arising during the policy period.

Businesses have increasingly shifted the economic consequences of environmental risks to their insurance carriers. For CGL policies written anywhere up to the late 1960's, few environmental exclusions exist. From the early 1970's through the mid-1980's, carriers used "sudden and accidental" exclusions to avoid pollution-related claims. After 1986, the entire insurance industry turned to "absolute" pollution exclusions.

Insurers' main argument to avoid paying environmental claims is that releases of hazardous substances are not "damages, property damage, or occurrences" as defined in their policies. Courts construe insurance policies liberally in favor of the insured. Thus, many courts require the carriers to provide a defense, and possibly indemnities, under certain older policies.[223] Companies must explore all their insurance policies when dealing with environmental contamination. As a practical matter, they should keep all insurance-related material, no matter how old.

---

[222] Historical information adapted from: Susan M. Cooke, The Law of Hazardous Waste, supra. (1995).

[223] Many courts have rendered key decisions holding that insurance companies had to pay for certain environmental contamination as "damages" under their policies and that the burden was on the insurance companies to provide a defense until they could prove no possible factual or legal basis for indemnity coverage. See, e.g., Villa Charlotte Bronte, Inc. v. Commercial Union Insurance Co., 64 N.Y.2d 846 (1985); Montrose Chemical Corp. v. Superior Court, 6 Cal. 4th 287 (1993); AIU Ins. Co. v. Superior Court, 28 Cal.App.4th 399 (1990).

In October 1995, Standard & Poor's (S&P) Ratings Group revised the insurance industry's environmental exposure estimate downward.[224] The cost projection for cleaning up of non-federal U.S. sites is $125 billion in total over the next 30 years. This is significantly less than the $165 billion over 30 year costs estimated in 1994 in two highly regarded studies. The reduction occurred because insurers are increasingly using out-of-court settlements, negotiating more favorable settlements, natural resources restoration claims have not materialized as expected, cleanup standards are being relaxed in some cases, and cleanup technology is improving and becoming less expensive. At the end of 1995, carriers' existing reserves for pollution claims total less than $30 billion, and there are 27 companies having shortfalls equal to one-third of their net worth.

b.   New Policies Available

Carriers continue to introduce insurance products tailored to environmental risks. The following list sets forth several categories of modern environmental insurance products: [225]

- <u>Pollution Legal Liability</u> - protects fixed sites in any industry with a pollution exposure. For example, manufacturing, waste management, petrochemicals, mining, etc.

- <u>Prospective First Party Clean Up</u> - provided in various degrees to a wide range of properties ranging from commercial real estate to industrial sites. This covers losses arising from ongoing operations on the insured's own property.

- <u>Retrospective First Party Pollution Clean Up</u> - covers preexisting pollution conditions not detected in a Phase I environmental audit and discovered during policy period. This targets commercial real estate and industrial sites.

- <u>Non-Owned Disposal Site Coverage</u> - provides coverages for off-site cleanup costs incurred at a waste disposal site, for example due to Superfund liability.

---

[224] Input into this section includes material from: Geraghty & Miller, <u>The Groundwater Newsletter</u>, Vol. 24, No. 21, p. 5 (Nov. 15, 1995).

[225] Courtesy of: Gregory E. Schilz, Vice President, Marsh & McLennan (San Francisco, 415/393-8172).

- <u>Owner Spill Liability</u> - targets generators of waste and manufacturers of products that can pose an environmental risk during transportation.

- <u>Underground Storage Tank Liability</u> - targets owners and operators of petroleum product tanks that need to comply with EPA financial responsibility requirements.

- <u>Excess Remediation Insurance</u> - provides coverage for remediation projects in the event the final costs exceed initial projections.

- <u>Contractors Pollution Liability</u> - targets not only environmental contractors (hazardous waste remediation and lead/asbestos abatement), but construction contractors including both trade contractors and general contractors.

(1)   What to Look for When Purchasing

Understanding and purchasing environmental liability policies can be very complex. A business needs to know how its insurance works, especially as it relates to pollution. Over the years, expensive policies have been issued that offered virtually no real environmental insurance coverage.[226] Unless an organization has a full-time risk manager, a knowledgeable broker can be instrumental. Purchasers should consider some factors when buying:[227]

- <u>Which policy is right?</u> Since each organization has different pollution exposures, one needs to decide the risks faced, decide which exposures to insure, and match such to the policies offered by the insurers. In addition, non-traditional insurance alternatives

---

[226] *See*, E.C. Brown, "What Lawyers Need to Know About Asbestos," <u>ABA Journal</u> (November, 1986).

[227] Courtesy of: Michael J. Grant, C.P.A., Account Executive, Complete Energy and Marine Insurance (Newport Beach, California, 714/263-0606). Prior to entering the insurance industry, Mr. Grant was the Chief Financial Officer of an environmental consulting and remediation contractor.

include captive insurers, risk retention groups, large deductible plans, retrospective rating plans, stop loss programs, and more.

- <u>What does the policy cover?</u> The insurance policy will specifically identify those costs covered by the policy. Most pollution policies pay those sums the business becomes legally obligated to pay for: claims related to bodily injury, property damage and cleanup (including defense). These policies provide coverage unless specifically excluded.

- <u>What is the policy limit?</u> The policy limit is the maximum amount that the insurer will pay related to <u>all</u> claims during the policy period. Once they exceed this limit, the business will be responsible for all further amounts.

- <u>Is the policy a claims-made or occurrence form?</u> A claims-made policy provides coverage for claims asserted against the company during the policy period, typically independent of whether the liability-imposing cause occurred during or before the policy period. Carriers generally write pollution policies on a claims-made form. An occurrence policy provides coverage for losses from a liability-imposing cause that occurred during the policy period, despite when the insured asserts the claim.

- <u>Is there a retroactive date in the policy?</u> The retroactive date is an additional provision within many claims-made policy forms. This date defines when coverage begins. As such, the insurance would not cover any liability-imposing cause that occurred before this date (even if the insured files the claim in the policy period). This date is generally the policy inception date.

- <u>What is the deductible or self-insured retention?</u> Most policies have a deductible or self-insured retention ("SIR"). A deductible is the amount paid when a loss occurs. A SIR operates similarly to a deductible except that the business maintains "control" of the claim (i.e., hires legal counsel to handle the claim) until they exhaust the SIR limit. Once they exhaust the SIR limit, the insurer takes charge of the claim. Usually, they will replace the original legal counsel with their own and continue with the claim.

- <u>How will the carrier make payment?</u> Most policies provide for the insurer to pay all sums that the insured become legally obligated to pay (in excess of the deductible or self-insured retention). Other policies require the insured to make those payments first.

- <u>Who is the insurance carrier?</u> This is just as important as choosing the right policy. Should the business have a claim, the insurer must have the financial strength and expertise to handle the claim. Many organizations evaluate the financial strength of insurance companies. The most commonly referenced is A.M. Best Company. Best rates insurers on their financial condition and operating performance (scale from A++ to F) and on their policyholder surplus or reserves (scale from 15 to 1). A++ 15 is the highest available rating.[228]

Brokers and insurers provide various underwriting services such as loss control, risk evaluations, and claims handling.[229] The insurance carrier generally provides loss control at no cost and includes such features as site inspections, determination of risk, and advice on minimization of exposure. The insurer, the broker, or an independent environmental engineering consulting firm can provide risk evaluation. The insurer will know exactly what it is looking for and will usually require the risk evaluation to bind coverage. The broker can provide a more independent risk evaluation and should have a separate division specializing in loss control and risk evaluation. Cost for evaluation by an independent firm can be expensive (preliminary evaluations may be $1,500, with complete evaluations costing $3,000 to $5,000), but worth it in the right situation.

The <u>coverage trigger</u> refers to the item that carriers recognize as a valid claim. For example, will a mere allegation cause the insurance company to become involved, or will they require written demands or a lawsuit?

---

[228] In addition to the letter grade, there may be a rating qualifier in the form of a small letter next to the capital letter grade. For example, a "w" means that a company may be exposed to a possible legal, financial, or market situation which could adversely affect its performance; an "e" indicates that the letter grade is that of the parent company. All the rating qualifiers are explained in the same introductory section as the ratings.

[229] Researched and drafted by: David Bowls, actuarial consultant and law student at Western State University College of Law (Irvine, California).

A retroactive date excludes events from being covered by the policy if the event occurred before the retroactive date. A typical retroactive date would be one year before the policy inception date. Thus, they would not cover an event unless it occurred within a year of the policy inception. Because of the difficulty of timing pollution events, it has become standard not to have a retroactive date. Carriers call such a policy a "full prior acts" policy, i.e., no cut off dates exist for prior occurrences. Of course, such a policy is likely to be more expensive but possibly advantageous.

An extended reporting period, also known as tail coverage, may be available that will cover events that occurred during the policy effective period but that the insured does not promptly report. Such an option excludes events occurring during the policy period that the insured does not report within the extended period.

Finally, special insurance may be necessary to fulfill the RCRA-imposed financial responsibility requirement on owners or operators of hazardous waste treatment, storage, or disposal facilities.[230] RCRA requires liability coverage with limits of $1 million per occurrence. This coverage must also have an annual aggregate of $2 million. RCRA requires policy limits of $3 million per occurrence, with an annual aggregate of $6 million, for owners and operators of the following units managing hazardous wastes: surface impoundment, landfill, land treatment, and disposal facilities. Owners and operators may show proper coverage by the following: insurance policy endorsement, financial ability, a letter of credit, surety bond, trust fund, or a combination of these subject to conditions.

(2)   Pricing

Frequency is the rate at which events are likely to occur. Severity is the seriousness or likely amount of damage when an event does occur. Coverage with low frequency and severity should be less expensive than a coverage whose frequency and severity are higher.

Pollution events occur infrequently, but the potential harm is large. Thus, actuarial analyses are based upon scarce data.[231] The result is variable pricing. Premiums are generally proportional to the size of the company modified by risk factors. Depending on the insurer and type of coverage,

---

[230] 40 C.F.R. §§ 264.147, 265.147.

[231] Prepared by David Bowls, supra.

this rating system may substantially affect the premium. For example, an insurer might look at the physical condition of a facility or the company managed operations and assign scores for various attributes. Ultimately, the carrier considers the deductible level and then applies a formula to help determine premiums.

Carriers often state coverage limits, or the maximum payment amount, as "per occurrence" often with an "aggregate" maximum payment for the policy. For example, a $10 million/$50 million limit allows $10 million for each occurrence with $50 million in aggregate coverage. The effect of higher limits is to raise the premium amount. The effect is nonlinear, however, so that the cost per dollar amount of coverage becomes cheaper as the carrier raises the limits. It is often a better bargain for the insured to buy coverage at a higher limit.

For a policy with a $25,000 deductible, and a $1 million limit, the expected minimum premium is $17,000 to $25,000. If the policy were under a combined general liability/pollution form, then the minimum would be about $35,000. If a group of insureds presented itself to a carrier, and all had similar operations with similar exposures, these minimum premiums could be lower, perhaps to the $10,000 range. Pricing for comparable coverages can typically vary by a factor of four[232] sometimes ranging from $1 to $20, for each $1000 of coverage (a factor of twenty).

4.   Bankruptcy

Bankruptcy is an imperfect risk management strategy for environmentally troubled companies.[233] The first objective of the bankruptcy system is to achieve an equitable distribution of the debtor's assets among its creditors. The second objective is to relieve the honest but unfortunate debtors from the weight of oppressive indebtedness. While bankruptcy is not a perfect defense to environmental liability, it allows short term avoidance of payments from such liability. Although courts across the country are giving environmental laws the broadest possible impact, high profile cases have reenforced the

---

[232] Martin T. Katzman, Chemical Catastrophes (1985).

[233] Adapted in part from: Roy B. True, Environmental Liability in Bankruptcy (1995).

longstanding primary status of bankruptcy policies.[234] This conflict between the goals of bankruptcy and environmental laws is a "battle of the titans."

a.   Dischargeability

A discharge in bankruptcy relieves the debtor from all debts that arose before bankruptcy, i.e., gives a fresh start. A debt is a liability on a claim.[235] While the law remains unclear on precisely which environmental obligations are claims, courts consider two main factors in deciding: 1) Is the obligation a right to payment? and 2) When did the claim arise?

The United States Supreme Court has held that cleanup orders are dischargeable since they are the equivalent of a monetary payment within the bankruptcy definition of claim.[236] Accordingly, the party facing a cleanup order may file a bankruptcy petition in federal court and be relieved of financial liability regarding the environmental claims.

The 9th Circuit has discharged cleanup liability in a Chapter 7 bankruptcy (liquidation as opposed to reorganization) since the agency's claim arose "at the time of actual or threatened release of the hazardous waste, or based upon the debtors' conduct."[237] In a relevant New York case, the court reached a similar result. It held that if "any" pre-petition triggering event occurs, e.g., release or threatened release, then the entire claim is dischargeable (though

---

[234] *E.g.*, the court in In re Jensen, 127 B.R. 27 (Bankr. 9th Cir. 1991), U.S. Bankruptcy Appellate Panel, cited In re Dant & Russell, 853 F.2d 700 (9th Cir. 1988), holding that environmental concerns "may not control the Bankruptcy Code in the absence of clear legislative intent."

[235] For bankruptcy purposes, defined to include a "right to payment." 11 U.S.C. § 101(5)(A)

[236] Ohio v. Kovacs, 469 U.S. 274 (1985). *See also*, United States v. Whizco, 841 F.2d 147, 150 (6th Cir. 1988) and In re Robinson, 46 B.R. 136, 139 (Bankr. M.D. Fla 1985), which have both similarly held that environmental obligations are dischargeable because the restoration sought was only possible with expenditure of money.

[237] In re Jensen, supra., where the court here followed In re Johns-Mansville, 57 B.R. 680 (Bankr. S.D.N.Y. 1986), an asbestos case, in adopting the expansive "debtor conduct" logic. Under this holding, all pre-petition liability is discharged.

90

the vast majority of wrongful acts occurred post-petition).[238] This decision affirms the In re Jensen, supra., pronouncement that bankruptcy law takes precedence over government environmental claims, absent a Congressional readjustment of priorities. However, the discharge may not relieve the principals or insurers of the corporation from liability.

b.   Automatic Stay

Once filed, the bankruptcy petition serves to automatically stay nearly all other actions against the debtor (discharger). However, the Bankruptcy Code sets forth two key exceptions to the automatic stay: (a) the government commencing or continuing action to enforce police or regulatory power, and (b) the government seeking to enforce a judgment, other than money, obtained in action to enforce police or regulatory power.[239]

In another New York case involving Exxon, the court applied the above exception. It held a bankruptcy stay did not shield the oil company since the City of New York's private cost recovery action under CERCLA §107 fell within the "police and regulatory power" exception.[240] In so holding, the court disregarded a technically sound argument that a mere city's actions should not qualify for the governmental enforcement exception because under CERCLA only state and federal actions are considered "governmental."[241]

---

[238] In re Chateaugay Corp. ("LTV"), 112 B.R. 513 (Bankr. S.D.N.Y. 1990).

[239] Bankruptcy Code § 362. It is worthy to note that environmental protection is specifically enumerated in the legislative history of this section as one of the potential exceptions to the automatic stay.

[240] City of New York v. Exxon Corp., No. 90-7360, 2nd Cir (May 2, 1991).

[241] The court instead found that since the Bankruptcy Code makes no distinctions in this regard, any level of government is entitled to the exception. Id. The key question which arises from the Exxon holding is whether courts will expand this approach to true private individuals or companies which are bringing CERCLA private causes of action. In so holding, a court would have to find that by bringing such an action the private litigants "stand in the shoes" of governmental bodies ordinarily entitled to the

c. Abandonment of Contaminated Property

The Bankruptcy Code provides that a trustee in bankruptcy, (or) the debtor in possession, may abandon property that is "burdensome."[242] In the seminal case of Midlantic,[243] the United States Supreme Court refused to allow a trustee to abandon contaminated property, stating that they must either sell it or clean it up, subject to several exceptions: (a) the environment law at issue is so onerous as to interfere with the bankruptcy adjudication itself; (b) the law is not reasonably designed to protect public health; or (c) the abandonment has no immediate threat to the environment.

Subsequently, various courts have both applied and rejected the Midlantic exceptions. In one such case, the court allowed a trustee to abandon part of a former oil refinery. It found no threat of immediate harm to public (despite the state agency's arguments to the contrary).[244] The court interpreted Midlantic to require merely that the bankruptcy court consider, but not be strictly bound by, state environmental laws. However, a different court subsequently contradicted in part Midlantic's central holding by refusing to allow a trustee abandonment of a hazardous waste site, though cleanup costs exceeded the assets of the estate.[245] The court in this latter case found that CERCLA imposed an implicit duty on the trustee to expend all unencumbered assets in cleaning up the site.

d. Administrative Priority

The Bankruptcy Code gives payment priority during bankruptcy to "administrative expenses," comprising all "actual, necessary costs and expenses of preserving the estate."[246] The cases are presently split on the

---

stay exception.

[242] Bankruptcy Code § 554.

[243] Midlantic Nat'l. Bank v. New Jersey Dept. of Envtl. Protec., 474 U.S. 494 (1986).

[244] In re Oklahoma Refining, 63 B.R. 562 (Bankr. W.D. Oklahoma 1986).

[245] In re Peerless Plating, 70 B.R. 943 (Bankr. W.D. Michigan 1987).

[246] Bankruptcy Code § 503.

question of whether environmental cleanup costs should be entitled to administrative priority.[247]

---

[247] For example: 1) <u>In re T.P. Long Chemical Inc.</u>, 45 Bankr. 278 (B.R. N.D. Ohio 1985): Yes administrative expenses since estate couldn't avoid CERCLA liability; 2) <u>Chicago, Rock Island & Pacific R.R.</u>, 756 F.2d 517 (7th Cir. 1985): No administrative expenses since benefit to estate too slight and indirect; 3) <u>In re Wall Tube & Metal Products Co.</u>, 831 F.2d 118, 123 (6th Cir. 1987): Yes administrative expenses (state stepped in because trustee wasn't complying with hazardous waste laws); and 4) <u>In re Dant & Russell, Inc.</u>, 853 F.2d 700, 709 (9th Cir. 1988): No administrative expenses since claim for reimbursement arose pre-petition.

CHAPTER 9
HAZARDOUS WASTE MINIMIZATION

Hazardous waste minimization is required by law.[248] For example, every signature on a Uniform Hazardous Waste Manifest by a large quantity generator certifies: "I have a program in place to reduce the volume and toxicity of waste generated."[249] For small quantity generators, the same signature certifies: "I have made a good faith effort to minimize my waste generator and select the best waste management method that is available to me and that I can afford."[250]

Reducing hazardous waste is a prudent part of every facility's strategy and should save money in the following ways:[251]

- Eliminate
  - Hazardous waste disposal costs and generator taxes
  - Treatment costs (e.g., water and energy)
  - Tail generator liability (e.g., landfill contamination)
- Decrease
  - Insurance costs
  - Transportation costs
  - Worker health problems and injuries
  - On-site pollution control and treatment costs
  - Record keeping

---

[248] Julia E. Kress, Esq. wrote this chapter.

[249] *Uniform Hazardous Waste Manifest*, "Generator's Certification," attached as Appendix "T" (discussed in detail in Chapter 10).

[250] Id.

[251] This chapter includes materials from: Facility Pollution Prevention Guide, U.S. EPA (May 1992); Daniel S. Witkowsky, Pollution Prevention in Mining and Mineral Processing Waste Assessments, U.S. Dept. of the Interior and U.S. Bureau of Mines, (1995); and Hazardous Waste Reduction: A Step-by-Step Guidebook for California Cities, Cal-EPA (June 1992).

A.   Getting Key Personnel Involved

New attitudes are critical for successful waste minimization programs. Every employee must have such minimizations as part of their job. The primary goal is to <u>prevent the creation of hazardous waste</u>, rather than just controlling it after generation.

Management must also be committed to the program. One way to accomplish this is by explaining the bottom-line benefits, i.e., cost savings. After management allocates resources to carry out the plan, plant personnel have an increased likelihood of paralleling the company's commitment. Management needs to provide a written endorsement of the program describing specific economic, public, human health, and environmental benefits. Written statements should also detail how the program will simplify regulatory compliance. If the company does not generate hazardous waste, the employees will not have to manage it. A Policy Statement and Implementation Plan should also set forth specific goals and identify the people responsible for following through.

Training and education are important motivational tools. Employees are highly familiar with waste problems. Thus, they often greet waste reduction programs with enthusiasm. Participation can be rewarding when helping the environment and saving money are the goals.

Employee recognition is a good motivator. For example, personnel who have made successful suggestions can be honored at staff meetings and in newsletters or press releases. In addition, the company can put a hazardous waste minimization employee of the year program in place (including posting pictures and names). Employee incentive programs are also a good way to encourage active involvement. Small monetary awards or compensatory time-off should boost morale for successful waste reduction ideas.

Incentive programs can also be directed at the department level. This is done on a larger scale and can encourage positive competition among departments. For instance, the business can give a lunch or dinner party for the department with the highest hazardous waste reduction over a six-month period. Another alternative is giving monthly awards to the department with the greatest minimization.

B.   Waste Minimization Group

The company needs to select key employees for a "Waste Minimization Group" who will initiate, evaluate, carry out, and maintain the plan.

Determining the size of the group is dependant upon scope and complexity of the operations. The makeup of the team is ideally a combination of company staff and outside professionals. The company should include employees who manage operations and who do waste-intensive tasks.

The organizers should consider the needs and problems of each department. They will be more receptive to any resulting changes if their department has been involved from the beginning. The community can become involved through interviews, touting the hazardous waste reduction program, on-site facility tours, advertising, direct mail, surveys, opinion polls, and/or open meetings (all of which boost public image of the company).

The Waste Minimization Group must be given specific responsibility, authority and goals. One person should be designated the group's leader who can keep the program moving in a direction that will guarantee that the hazardous waste reduction program works. This leader must have "people" skills, the ability to understand positive and negative information, and credibility within the company to reduce friction from other employees.

C.   Plan Objectives

The objectives of any hazardous waste minimization plan should include the following:

- Identifying all hazardous waste generated at the facility
- Determining the processes that contribute the greatest amount of wastes
- Evaluating processes as candidates for source reduction or minimization
- Determining appropriate alternatives for each process
- Implementing the highest benefit alternatives

D.   Facility/Hazardous Waste Assessment

The Hazardous Waste Group performs an assessment of the facility's current operations to gather the background information. Such activities should be done under the direction of knowledgeable attorneys in order to best secure attorney confidentiality protection for the results.[252]

The *Assessing Current Facility Operations Checklist* and *Facility Information Worksheet*, respectively attached as Appendices "H" and "I," can help in doing the assessment. The group must assess waste streams to decide on reduction methods. The *Characterizing Individual Waste Streams Worksheet*, attached as Appendix "J," should similarly help a facility complete such an evaluation. The group should review any existing site evaluations and other data concerning waste streams. This would include a review of the inventory and usage of substances that create hazardous waste.

Depending upon the size of the facility, creating a separate "Waste Assessment Team" may be necessary. Any such team should include at least one member from the Waste Minimization Group. An ideal team mix would be an engineer, a manager, a line worker, an environmental specialist, an accountant, and a purchaser.

The group should clearly characterize materials that are put into the processes. The *Description of Input Materials Worksheet*, attached as Appendix "K," facilitates analysis of material usage. Reviewing the day-to-day operating records, permits, and regulatory reports can help locate this information. If it is an older facility, historical records like newspaper articles and photographs may also help.

The group should plan a site visit well in advance. The tour should have specific goals and be done on a day that is typical of the facility's day-to-day operation. Such an inspection is necessary to verify the data used, identify issues not adequately documented, and determine new areas to assess. They can photograph or videotape operations, being careful to maximize the ability to keep such information confidential (e.g., under the attorney confidentiality doctrines or emerging self-audit protections). The photo or videotape may come in handy later for showing any before and after improvements. Visiting the site several times to see different processes at different shifts and under various conditions may be necessary.

Employee interviews can be good for filling in missing data and to solicit suggestions. Typical areas to question relate to procedures for material purchasing, storage, waste collection, administrative control, and costs. They

---

[252] *See* "Attorney Confidentiality" in Chapter 7 (Contaminated Properties), and "Attorney Confidentiality Protection for Audits" in Chapter 8 (Environmental Risk Management).

should carefully detail all housekeeping practices, spills, cleanup and leak control problems. The group should note any equipment that is leaking and any odors and/or fumes and the overall cleanliness of the facility. The team should also examine any discrepancies between actual operations and operating manuals.

E.   Prioritizing Wastes to Minimize

The group must next rank hazardous wastes to reduce. The goal is to identify the biggest sources of waste generation and to understand how to minimize them. Creating a flow chart of processes can help. The chart will identify the best target steps in the process, i.e., where it creates the bulk of waste or uses the most raw materials like energy and water.

Intuitively, the group should tackle the largest waste streams first. Rankings should take into account volume, cost of handling/disposal, and toxicity. The latter, however, can be difficult since it may involve more "professional judgment" and may not directly result in cost savings. In fact, ranking the waste by the cost of treatment and disposal usually factors in the relative risk of the wastes since more toxic wastes are generally more expensive to manage and dispose. Other factors that may come into play during the cost-benefit analysis are:

- Compliance with current federal, state and local government requirements
- Potential recovery of valuable byproducts
- Reduction in energy use
- Available budgets

F.   Reduction Alternatives

The following examples are potential ways that a facility can reduce the amount of hazardous waste used or generated in its processes.

1.   Changing Housekeeping or Inventory Controls

Using housekeeping and inventory controls to minimize hazardous waste is advantageous to a facility for the following reasons:

- Easy to implement and cost effective

99

- Reduces the amount of material used, resulting in less waste
- Decreases the chance of any accidental spills, leaks, and worker injury
- Simplifies the preparation of the hazardous waste manifests

a. Areas for Waste Accumulations

If areas are designated for waste accumulation, and staff properly label the containers, the company can avoid mixing different waste types (including hazardous and nonhazardous). The group should train employees to use containers and should know the importance of keeping different wastes separated. For example, they should not mix oily waste with solvent-containing waste and they should not throw ordinary trash away in hazardous waste accumulation containers. All hazardous waste accumulation containers should always be kept covered and the surrounding areas should be clean and uncluttered.

b. Areas for Virgin Materials Storage

The hazardous materials "virgin" storage area should be different from the hazardous waste accumulation area. When not actively using hazardous materials, employees should return them immediately to a designated storage area. In addition, the storage area should have separate areas for different kinds of chemicals. For example, workers should store solvents in an area separate from flammable materials. Keeping all containers closed should avoid potential spills or contamination of hazardous materials. Material safety data sheets should be available near the point of storage for all hazardous materials.

c. Use of Current Inventory

Employees should inspect all material storage areas monthly to ensure that they remove materials no longer being used. Materials that pass their expiration date should be considered waste and should be properly disposed.[253] They should also make a review to see if materials are expiring before use. Sometimes bulk ordering appears cost-effective. Yet, if the facility is disposing expired materials, buying in bulk is not achieving its goal.

---

[253] Prior to disposing materials, consider whether there is a specific business that can use the remaining materials. State agencies often have lists of potential users for ready-to-discard hazardous materials.

d.   Complete Usage Before Disposal

Staff should not discard hazardous materials until they are expired or gone. For example, they should not discard rags until they can no longer use them effectively. Employees should also refrain from tossing degreasing solvents until they no longer effectively clean products. They should only open one container of material at a time. When this is empty, then the workers can open a new container.

2.   Substituting Less Hazardous/Nonhazardous Materials

This alternative to reduce the amount of hazardous waste generated will be easy to carry out where practical substitutions exist. First, they should list suitable less hazardous and/or nonhazardous materials. In determining if a substitute material can replace a hazardous one, the group should ask if it will:

• Work as well?[254]
• Violate equipment/maintenance specifications?
• Result in a different type of waste stream or release?
• Cost more (e.g., require additional equipment/maintenance)?
• Pose a problem to regulatory authorities?

Using appropriate substitutes will generate less hazardous waste, lower disposal costs, and decrease worker injuries. Other considerations, when substituting materials include the fact that aqueous solutions may require a large amount of agitation. This may require equipment modifications. Different processing times may also happen with substitutions (e.g., increased drying times for less volatile materials).

---

[254] For example, water based detergents and surfactants can be effective in replacing solvents for many heavy duty cleaning applications, such as removing greases and oil from parts, as well as performing general housekeeping such as washing greasy floors, walls, etc. Sometimes washing the parts with high pressure hot or cold water or steam will work as effectively as solvents.

3. Recycling

The company can carry out two types of recycling. For on-site recycling, the goal is to use the otherwise problematic hazardous item as a raw material in one of the facility's processes. Typically on-site recycling involves purchasing some equipment and additional personnel. This investment may prove worthwhile at a facility depending on the amount of hazardous waste that they can recycle. Recycling on-site can produce the following benefits: reduced off-site transportation liability, elimination of manifesting, reduced raw material costs, and reducing disposal costs. Disadvantages of this approach include: potential waste facility permitting, increased worker exposure, and increased potential for a release due to handling in multiple processes.

Off-site recycling has the following advantages: typically no additional labor or equipment, possibly round-tripping (where the recycling facility returns prior loads of recycled material for reuse), and possibly reduced costs (versus straight disposal). Negative considerations for off-site disposal include: increased transportation liability and manifesting. While off-site recycling is supposed to reduce "tail" generator liability, it does not in all situations. Take for example the infamous Yakima site in Washington State. For a decade or so, Yakima was a key national destination for recycling the chlorinated solvent PCE (perchloroethylene). When the drinking water became contaminated at Yakima, the site itself became a Washington State cleanup priority. Ultimately the cleanup authority pursued every generator who sent materials to Yakima for a volumetric share of CERCLA-type response costs.

4. Eliminating Certain Processes

The objective behind this hazardous waste minimization alternative is to eliminate any unnecessary processes that generate hazardous waste. This is probably the hardest alternative to set up since most of the facility's processes are probably necessary to its daily operations. However, it may prove worthwhile to analyze some routine operations where the operator may change frequencies. For example, does the facility change the oil on all pieces of equipment (whether necessary or not)?

G. Feasibility Evaluation

For each potential option, the group should evaluate its feasibility. To help in this endeavor, the *Options for Minimizing Hazardous Waste Worksheet* and the *Description of a Specific Waste Minimization Option Worksheet* are respectively attached as Appendices "L" and "M." These worksheets should be completed using creative brainstorming to help determine the best alternatives. The final decision may even require testing. For example, they may need to test any material substitution to see if it really will work as well as the original.

Hazardous waste reductions generally fall into one of three categories:

- Equipment
- Personnel/procedures
- Materials

At this point, the waste reduction alternatives should be ranked using technical, environmental and economic feasibility analysis. To help evaluate these aspects for proposed alternatives, please use the various *Feasibility Worksheets* (e.g., equipment, personnel/procedure, and materials), collectively attached as Appendix "N."

The company must address the economic feasibility of any alternative. The cost of setting up a change at the facility is only seen up-front. Therefore, estimating the savings must evaluate long term benefits. Yet, the additional costs of continuing to dispose of hazardous wastes can be very hard to calculate. Such figures include potential fines as well as projected costs of future cleanups and litigation. Using the *Cost Estimation Worksheets* (e.g., operating costs, capital costs, and profitability), collectively attached as Appendix "O," may help in doing such estimations.

H.   Implementation/Maintenance

The group must consider certain considerations before starting the plan. For example, a facility may have to:

- Purchase new equipment and materials
- Change current purchasing procedures
- Develop and submit new annual and capital improvement budgets
- Initiate the bidding procedure for capital purchases
- Train employees on new procedures or equipment
- Develop a phased approach for introducing new methods and materials

A schedule should be prepared with milestones contained in each phase, from implementation to yearly goals. Choosing specific target dates to help quantify each goal is important and facilitates the company's commitment to carry out those goals. This also gives the facility a way to measure its progress. These quantitative goals may be difficult to prepare but will in the end be valuable.

Carrying out the program should include at a minimum:

- Estimating the costs of the start up and expected pay-back period
- Appointing a coordinator to track the minimization plan's progress
- Measuring performance against goals
- Modifying the schedule based on the ongoing program tracking
- Communicating progress to management and employees

The group should then evaluate progress quarterly and monitor the plan to see if they are meeting objectives and, if not, to provide ideas on modifications. If the plan is not meeting the objectives, they should adjust the hazardous waste minimization program. If the plan is meeting objectives, then the company needs to be aware of it so that they can put credit where it is due.

CHAPTER 10
TRANSPORTATION OF HAZARDOUS MATERIALS

U.S. law requires that all hazardous materials transportation comply with regulations for proper identification, packaging, and documentation (e.g., manifesting).[255] Failure to follow these laws subjects generators and transporters to civil and criminal prosecution. This chapter describes key laws and Department of Transportation ("DOT") regulations governing the transport of hazardous materials.

A.   Labeling

Unless an exemption applies, the label for the transportation of any hazardous material must contain the following specific written information: (a) the proper shipping name, (b) the hazard class of the material, (c) the United Nations ("UN") identification number, and (d) any hazards that the materials present.[256] The shipper must also mark the package with the person shipping the package or the person who will be receiving the package.

For help in determining the proper shipping name, please use the federal *C.F.R. Hazardous Materials Table*, attached in part as Appendix "P."[257] The *Table* includes the hazard class, UN identification number, and identifies specific hazard warnings that the label must contain (e.g., corrosive, flammable, etc.).

The hazard warning on the label must look exactly as pictured in the *C.F.R. Hazardous Warning Label Examples*, attached as Appendix "Q."[258] The label must be durable, weather resistant, and able to withstand 30-day exposure to

---

[255] Julia E. Kress, Esq. authored this chapter.

[256] 49 C.F.R. § 172.301.

[257] The *Hazardous Materials Table* is located at 49 C.F.R. § 172.101.

[258] 49 C.F.R. §§ 172.407(b) and 172.442.

any encountered conditions.[259] The shipper must print on or fix the label to the top or the side of the container of hazardous materials. If the container is a cylinder, has an irregular surface, or is too small for the label, then such may be placed on an attached tag.[260]

As an example, a common substance in the precious metals industry is spent potassium gold cyanide bath containing gold in solution.[261] A partial list of the current U.S. domestic shipping requirements for this material is as follows:

Material Description:	Potassium Cyanide Solution, 6.1, UN1680
Packing Group:	I
Hazard Labels (2):	Poison, Hazardous Waste

The *Sample Scenarios Regarding Transportation of Hazardous Materials to Reclaim Precious Metals*, attached as Appendix "R," provides eight additional examples for proposed off-site shipment of hazardous materials related to the precious metals industry.

B.   Packaging

Any person that offers the hazardous material for transportation must ensure that they have manufactured/assembled and marked it following DOT regulations.[262] One way to insure that a container meets these requirements is to obtain the packaging manufacturer's certification that the packaging meets DOT hazardous material regulations.[263]

Hazardous material packages must withstand minimum and maximum transportation temperatures. Also, no mixture of gases or vapors can occur within the package that may increase heat or pressure.[264] The shipper must

---

[259] Id. at §§ 172.407(a), (d)(3) and (d)(5).

[260] Id. at § 172.407(b).

[261] Adapted from: Charles S. Tatakis (Handy & Harman), "How to Get it from Here to There Correctly and Safely," IPMI Environmental Workshop (January 19-21, 1994, Arlington Virginia).

[262] 49 C.F.R. § 173.22(a).

[263] Id.

[264] Id. at § 173.24(b).

pay close attention to the possible corrosivity, permeability, softening, and premature aging of packages. They may not place hazardous and nonhazardous materials together within one outer package if the hazardous materials can react dangerously.[265] A package may contain more than one hazardous material when the inner and outer packaging complies independently with the regulations.[266]

To find the proper packaging for hazardous material, please consult the previously-mentioned *C.F.R. Hazardous Materials Table*,[267] attached as Appendix "P." The following columns of the *Table* apply:

- Column (5): packing group, by danger (I is high, II is medium, III is low)[268]
- Column (7): applicable "code" (e.g., B69, N74)[269]
- Column (8): exemption or bulk/non-bulk requirement[270]

---

[265] Id. at § 173.24 (e).

[266] Id. at § 173.24a (c).

[267] Id. at § 172.101.

[268] Hazardous materials that fall within hazard classes 2 and 7 and ORM-D materials ("other regulated material, class D", typically consumer waste) do not have packing groups. Also, if more than one packing group is indicated for a specific hazardous material, then regulations provide a separate method for differentiating between the groups. Id. at § 173, Subpart D.

[269] Id. at § 172.101(h). The meaning of each "code" contained in Column (7) is specified in the regulations at 49 C.F.R. § 172.102.

[270] Id. at § 172.101. The specific numbers set forth under each such column refers to applicable provisions of 49 C.F.R. § 173. For example, for potassium cyanide, Column 8B indicates 211 in the hazardous materials table. This means that to review the special packaging provisions applicable to potassium cyanide, one would look at 49 C.F.R. § 173.211. Any special packaging requirements are in addition to the general requirements applicable to all hazardous materials.

Packages must be closed such that they are secure and leak-proof.[271] The shipper may vent packages to reduce internal pressure when designed to allow such. However, this technique cannot allow hazardous materials to escape or where resulting gases are poisonous, likely to create a flammable mixture with the air, or is an asphyxiant.[272] The specific gravity of a hazardous material must not exceed that marked on the package or, if unmarked, a specific gravity of 1.2.[273]

Transportation of liquid hazardous materials all in one package must be with all closures facing upward. The shipper must also clearly mark the packages with orientation markings on two opposite vertical sides, showing arrows pointing in an upright direction.[274] This requirement does not apply to a package with inner containers consisting of cylinders.[275] Liquids that are transported must not completely fill a container at a temperature of 55° Celsius (131° Fahrenheit) or less.[276]

In multiple layer packages, they must design the outer package so that any friction that occurs during transportation does not generate enough heat to alter the hazardous material stability. The shipper must ensure the inner layers do not breach causing a release. Metallic items, such as nails and staples, must not protrude inside the outer package that may damage the inner layer.[277]

C.   Quantity Exceptions

There are two quantity exceptions from DOT requirements: small quantity and limited quantity (with total weight less than 30 kilograms for the latter).[278] The small quantity hazardous materials are exempt if they meet

---

[271] Id. at § 173.24 (f).

[272] Id. at § 173.24 (g).

[273] Id. at § 173.24a (b).

[274] Id. at §§ 172.32(a) and 173.249(a)(l).

[275] Id. at § 172.32(c).

[276] Id. at § 173.24a (d).

[277] Id. at § 173.24a (a).

[278] Id. at §§ 173.150-173.156.

the following requirements:

- No more than 30 milliliters (one liquid ounce)
- No opening or altering of packages in the stream of commerce
- The shipper certifies compliance by marking on the outside of the package: "This package conforms to conditions and limitations specified in 49 C.F.R. § 173.4"[279]

    D.   Notification of Regulated Waste Activity

After obtaining the required EPA identification number, all generators and transporters of hazardous <u>wastes</u> are to inform the EPA that they are conducting RCRA-regulated activities. They need to fill out the *Notification of Regulated Waste Activity* form, a copy of which is attached as Appendix "S." Once completed, the company must mail it to the applicable regional EPA office. They should immediately report any changes to information contained in the form to the EPA.

    E.   Required Documentation

        1.   Shipping Papers

The DOT requires that shipping papers accompany all hazardous materials.[280] If shipping hazardous wastes, then the parties must use a "hazardous waste manifest" (discussed below). The document must describe the hazardous material, including: shipping name, hazard class, UN identification number, packing group, and total quantity (by either net or gross).[281]

---

[279] <u>Id</u>. at § 173.4(a).

[280] The shipping paper can either be separate from the hazardous waste manifest, or if specific information is included on the manifest, DOT will not require a separate shipping paper. In order to only have the hazardous material being transported accompanied by the uniform hazardous waste manifest and not a separate shipping paper, the following information needs to be included on the manifest in the <u>specific order</u> indicated: (1) the proper shipping name, (2) the DOT hazard class, (3) the UN Identification Number, and (4) the Packing Group.

[281] <u>Id</u>. at § 172.202(a).

The shipping paper must also contain the total quantity of the hazardous material, the type of packing and destination[282] along with one of the following certifications:

> This is to certify that the above-named hazardous materials are properly classified, described, packaged, marked and labeled, and are in proper condition for transportation according to the applicable regulations of the Department of Transportation.
>
> [or]
>
> I hereby declare that the contents of this consignment are fully and accurately described above by proper shipping name and are classified, packed, marked and labeled, and are in all respects in proper condition for transport by [insert type of transportation] according to applicable international and national governmental regulations.[283]

2. Hazardous Waste Manifests[284]

Shipments of hazardous wastes fall under the hazardous waste manifest system.[285] California's version of the EPA's *Uniform Hazardous Waste Manifest*, is attached as Appendix "T." The law does not require a manifest, however, for generators who produce between 100 and 1,000 kilograms per month of hazardous waste if:

- There is waste reclamation by written contract
- The agreement contains the type of waste and number of shipments
- The reclaimer owns and operates the transporting vehicle
- The generator keeps the contract for three years after it expires

---

[282] Id. at § 172.202(c) (also noting that abbreviations can be used to express units of measurement and the types of packaging).

[283] Id. at § 172.204(a).

[284] Input into this section includes material from: Susan M. Cooke, The Law of Hazardous Waste: Management, Cleanup, Liability, and Litigation (Matthew Bender, 1995).

[285] 40 C.F.R. § 262.20(a).

The EPA has for several years been considering redefining "waste." The major provision of interest to the precious metals industry is a proposal that would create a <u>recycling manifest</u> for transport of materials and would remove secondary market precious metals from the hazardous waste transportation requirements.

a.   Required Information

The manifest must include: generator identification (e.g., name, address, telephone number, and EPA Identification Number), and waste DOT shipping name, hazard class, identification number, quantity, number and type of containers, and any special handling instructions. The generator must also designate a permitted facility for handling the specific waste and possibly one alternate transporter in an emergency. [286] If for some reason the transporter cannot deliver the waste to the primary facility, then the generator can designate either another facility or the transporter must return the waste to the generator. [287] The generator and transporter must sign the manifest by hand (i.e., no stamped signatures are allowed).

b.   Interstate Transportation

Most states use an adapted version of the EPA's *Uniform Hazardous Waste Manifest*. However, some states still issue their own manifest forms. When this is the case, the shipper must determine which state's manifest to use, following these guidelines:

- Mandatory use of any destination state manifest
- If no destination state manifest, then the generator state manifest
- If neither state has its own manifest, then the EPA's *Uniform Hazardous Waste Manifest*.[288]

---

[286] <u>Id</u>. at § 262.20(b) and (c).

[287] <u>Id</u>. at § 262.20 (d).

[288] <u>Id</u>. at § 262.21.

c.   Copies

The following all must end up with copies of the manifest: (a) the generator (including a post-shipment copy), (b) every transporter, and (c) the owner or operators of the destination facility.[289] For interstate transport to non-RCRA authorized states, the generator is responsible for ensuring the designated facility agrees to sign and return the manifest and that any out-of-state transporters sign and forward the manifest to that facility.[290]

If transport is by ship, the generator must provide three copies of the dated and signed manifest to the owner or operator of either the designated facility and if internationally, to the last water transporter to handle it in U.S. waters.[291] They need not send copies of the manifest to each "intermediary" transporter.

Transport by rail makes the generator responsible for sending at least three copies of the signed and dated manifest to the:

• Next non-rail transporter, if one exists
• Designated facility, if only by rail transport
• Last rail carrier handling the wastes (if shipped internationally)[292]

d.   Generator Certification

The manifest form requires that the generator complete two certifications. The first certification provides that the shipper has accurately described the waste and complied with other applicable requirements (including all international requirements). Second, the generator must sign a generator certification regarding waste minimization. Large quantity generators certify: "I have a program in place to reduce the volume and toxicity of waste generated." Small quantity generators certify: "I have made a good faith effort to minimize my waste generator and select the best waste management method that is available to me and that I can afford."

---

[289] Id. at § 262.23.

[290] Id. at § 262.23(e).

[291] Id.

[292] Id.

3.   Exception Report

Generators of more than 1,000 kilograms of hazardous waste per month have a special requirement. If after 35 days, the transporter and/or designated facility fail to return an executed copy of the manifest, the generator must contact them to decide the status of that shipment. If after 55 days they still have not given the generator the manifest, then the generator must fill out and submit an "exception report" to the EPA Regional Administrator. The exception report must attach a copy of the partially-executed manifest and describe efforts made to find the shipment.

Generators between 100 and 1,000 kilograms of hazardous waste per month, have 60 days to secure a copy of the fully executed manifest. If this does not occur, then the generator must submit a copy of the manifest to the EPA Regional Administrator showing no confirmation of waste delivery.

4.   Manifest Records Retention

When the generator receives a copy of the executed manifest from the designated facility, the generator must then retain it for at least three years. Generators who generate more than 1,000 kilograms of hazardous waste in a month must also retain their biennial reports and any exception reports for three years. The generator must also retain the results of any hazardous waste characterization testing for three years from the shipping date.

CHAPTER 11
EMERGENCY PREPAREDNESS

Industrial facilities, and all businesses face the possibility of catastrophic damage from natural events (e.g., floods and earthquakes) and accidents (e.g., fires, human error, and equipment failures).[293] Recent reminders of natural catastrophes include the earthquakes in Kobe, Japan (1995) and Northridge, California (1994), and the Mississippi Valley flood (1993). Dramatic accidental disasters also leave lasting images, such as the toxic cloud release at Union Carbide's facility in Bhopal, India and many train derailments worldwide. Companies should prepare for the worst of such disasters (and by definition lesser events) thereby reducing injuries (to people and the environment) and lost profits (from physical damage, downtime, and bad publicity).

Companies often ignore disaster preparedness until an emergency arises. For example, European industry greatly improved preparedness after a 1976 industrial accident at the Icmesa Chemical plant in Seveso, Italy. A reactor safety valve at the plant vented the toxic chemical dioxin (tetrachloro-dibenzodioxine, or "TCDD") into the atmosphere. Planning and communications were so poor that evacuation of the surrounding community did not begin for ten days. Although no deaths resulted, the accident put more than 220,000 people at risk. The Icmesa event shocked Europe and prompted the European Union's "Seveso Directive."[294] Industrial accidents, however, continue: In July, 1988 a gas compressor leak on the Pipe Alpha oil platform in the North Sea caused an explosion, killing 167 men.[295] Fortunately, businesses can best manage the risks and consequences of these disasters by advance emergency preparedness.

---

[293] Michael Paul Hutchins, Esq., P.E., authored this chapter.

[294] Nick Skeens, "The 'Worst-Case' Scenario," <u>Resources</u>, Vol. 17 (November 5, 1995). Europe is now replacing the Seveso Directive with the updated Control of Major Hazards (COMH) measure.

[295] <u>Id</u>.

A.   Preparing for a Disaster

1.   The Planning Team

The ideal planning team will include representatives from all areas of a
company's operations. A group, rather than one or two planners, will offer a
broad perspective on the issues, and enhance the stature of the planning
process. The group's representatives should include:

- Upper management
- Line management
- Labor
- Engineering and
  maintenance
- Environmental
- Legal

- Worker safety
- Human resources
- Finance and purchasing
- Public relations
- Security
- Sales and marketing

The planning group should have full authority to develop and set up the plan.
The company should establish a clear line of authority within the group. The
group should establish a mission statement, development schedule, and
budgets for research, printing, consulting services, seminars, and other
expenses early. A series of weekly meetings should maintain the momentum
of the project towards a six-week completion date.

2.   Analyzing Hazards and Capabilities

The planning team should conduct risk assessment through brainstorming
sessions. Governmental agencies, community response organizations and
utility companies are invaluable sources of information. The team should
evaluate temporary power outages, ruptured storage tanks, loss of power, and
natural catastrophic events. By preparing for the worst, a company will be
ready for less severe events. Professional disaster recovery consultants[296] and
public agencies can provide valuable insight.[297]

---

[296] A *Disaster Recovery Consultants List*, attached as Appendix "U," lists
consultants providing such services worldwide.

[297] The possible effects of a 7.0 earthquake along the Newport-Inglewood
fault zone (NIFZ) in Southern California has been developed in a 200 page
report by the California Department of Conservation, Division of Mines and
Geology. The *Planning Scenario, Newport -Inglewood Fault (Executive
Summary)* is attached as Appendix "V." A complete copy of this Special

a.   Critical Products and Services

An evaluation of critical products and services may suggest the need for backup. Lifeline services include electrical, water, sewer, gas, telecommunications, security and transportation. Prudent companies will also identify services and goods necessary to continue business operations during a crisis, especially those from sole source vendors. They may establish mutual aid agreements to guard against shortages of vital products and services.

b.   Internal Resources

The existing facilities, personnel and equipment should be evaluated for disaster remedies. As the structural safety of the building is paramount, analyzing code compliance is a first step.[298] Governmental agencies update codes periodically. They base these actions upon better scientific knowledge (e.g., for structure loading during catastrophic events). Typically, buildings need only meet the applicable building code(s) in effect <u>at the time of construction</u>. Upgrades to future code requirements are not necessary unless specifically required.

Thus, <u>many</u> existing industrial and commercial buildings could not meet current seismic codes if built today. In California, authorities will not deem a building a public nuisance because it does not conform to the current Uniform Building Code if it conforms to the code in effect at the time of

---

<u>Publication 99</u> can be obtained for $22.00 from the Division of Mines & Geology, Department of Conservation, P.O. Box 2980, Sacramento, CA 95812-2980.

[298] Specific building, safety, and hazardous materials codes are available from services such as Building News, Los Angeles, California (telephone: 800/873-6397), including:
  Uniform Building Code, BOCA National Building Code
  BOCA National Fire Prevention Code
  National Electric Code; National Electrical Safety Code
  Uniform Mechanical Code; BOCA National Building Code
  Uniform Plumbing Code; BOCA National Plumbing Code

construction.[299] Compliance with codes, however, does not ensure that a facility is "safe," nor does it necessarily protect the facility owner from legal liability.[300] Courts may impose negligence liability for failing to exercise the standard of care prevalent in a particular industry.

Detailed structural, piping and system evaluations should follow next. For example, in locations at risk of significant seismic activity, boilers and storage tanks should be secured against abrupt lateral and uplift forces. Similarly, in areas susceptible to flooding, companies should evaluate tanks for uplift forces from water. The Mississippi Valley flood of 1993 ripped multiple natural gas storage tanks from their foundations due to such a buoyancy effect, floating precariously for days, secured only by supply lines to the tanks.

Utility line security is also important. In Kobe, the 1995 earthquake destroyed or severely damaged more than 55,000 buildings, largely due to fires resulting from ruptured natural gas lines.[301] The fires destroyed more than one million square meters (255 acres) of urban and industrial property.[302] Tokyo guards against such an occurrence by using thousands of

---

[299] California Government Code § 65590(4). The Kansas Supreme Court found that there is no legal duty to rebuild in order to comply with updated building codes. Glynos v. Jagoda, 249 Kan. 473 (1991). Seattle Building Code § 103 provides the same. The California Education Code (§ 39140(b) 81130) provides that school fire damage repairs are acceptable if they comply with rules and building standards used for the original work. This provision, however, does not apply to wind or earthquake repairs. Id. at § 39140(b).

[300] The Kansas Supreme Court found that a property owner was liable for an occupant's injuries even though it complied with all applicable building codes. Glynos, supra. The Louisiana Court of Appeal affirmed a similar holding in Carpenter v. Hartford Fire Insurance Company and Jasper Haddad, 537 So.2d 1283 (1989). Courts have also imposed liability in spite of compliance with National Electrical Safety Code (NESC), Folks v. Kansas Power & Light, 243 Kan. 57 (1988), and National Fire Protection Association (NFPA) standards, Jones v. Hittle Service, Inc, 219 Kan. 627 (1976).

[301] "Event Report: Japan-The Great Hanshin Earthquake, January 17, 1995," Risk Management Solutions, Inc. and Failure Analysis Associates, Inc. (1995).

[302] Id.

motion detecting shut off valves throughout its gas distribution system.[303] Additionally, all residential gas meters in Tokyo are "smart meters," equipped with similar shut off valves.[304] In San Francisco, plans are under way to use semiconductor chips that trigger automobile air bags to shut down gas flow in a strong earthquake.[305]

Containment of hazardous materials is a special concern in disasters. Where fire risks are significant, materials for tanks, connectors, and pipelines should be heat resistant. Companies should use double-walled tanks, and secondary containment areas to prevent the escape of hazardous materials into the environment. Containment areas should have sufficient holding capacity to contain simultaneous releases from multiple tanks within the area. Ruptured electrical and water lines may also cause significant harm, particularly if a facility houses reactive chemicals.

Facility personnel are also critical. At the primary level, companies should have fire brigades, a hazardous materials response team, emergency medical services, security, management, and public relations. At a secondary level, to continue operations during disaster, the team should concentrate on: power, security, payroll, communications, production, customer services, shipping and receiving, and recovery support.

As experts better understand the forces of catastrophic events, and methods to safeguarding against them, more businesses are taking action. Legally, this raises the standard of care for all within the industry. The mere presence of an evacuation plan without full response contingencies for a worst case scenario may be of little use. It may not help in an emergency and will be an Achilles' heal in defense to legal liability for negligence.[306]

---

[303] "The Day the Earth Shook," Nova Broadcasting (January, 1996).

[304] Id.

[305] Id.

[306] In California a well established rule dictates that the amount of care taken (and thus the thoroughness of the plan) must be in proportion to the danger to be avoided and the consequences reasonably to be anticipated. Beck v. Sirota (1941) 42 Cal.App.2d 551.

c.　　External Resources

Companies may need many external resources in an emergency.[307]
Sometimes, formal agreements may be useful to define the facility's
relationship with the following:

• Fire department	• Contractors
• Hazardous materials responders	• Emergency equipment suppliers
• Emergency medical	• Insurance carriers
• Hospitals	• Private security companies
• Local and state police	
• Utilities	

Such agreements help ensure priority (e.g., with emergency equipment
suppliers and contractors) and avoid confusion or delay by public entities
(e.g., hazardous materials responders and police). Drafting an external
resources agreement can be tricky since they often involve broad ideas and,
by necessity, flexible approaches.

d.　　Vulnerability Assessment

Finally, the team prepares a vulnerability assessment to evaluate the
probability and potential impact of each emergency. Emergency preparedness
experts call this a quantified risk assessment. A *Vulnerability Analysis
Worksheet,* attached as Appendix "X," is helpful in assigning probabilities of
events, estimating impacts, and assessing resources using a numerical
system.[308] The higher the scores, the more a company needs disaster
planning.

To use the chart, list all emergencies that could affect a facility in the first
column, including those that could originate from within the facility and from
the surrounding community. Below are some factors to consider in listing
emergencies:

---

[307] A list of *Federal and State Emergency Management Agencies* is
attached as Appendix "W."

[308] The "Vulnerability Analysis Chart" was developed by the Federal
Emergency Management Agency and presented in its "Emergency
Management Guide for Business and Industry."

Historical Occurrences

- Fires
- Severe weather
- Hazardous material spills
- Transportation accidents
- Earthquakes
- Robbery and Theft

- Terrorism
- Hurricanes
- Utility outages
- Loss of Records
- Riots

Failures

- Safety
- Telecommunications
- Computers

- Power
- Heating/cooling
- Security

Human Error

- Poor training
- Poor maintenance
- Carelessness

- Misconduct
- Substance abuse
- Fatigue

Physical Facility

- Outdated or deficient construction
- Hazardous materials
- Combustibles
- Equipment layout

- Lighting
- Evacuation routes and exits
- Proximity of shelter areas
- Power and utility outages

After completing a list of potential emergencies, the team should note the relative likelihood of each occurrence in the probability column. This is both an objective and subjective process. Choosing a particular event may be helpful, with a known probability, as a baseline emergency. Other emergencies can them be rated relative to the baseline emergency.

Next, evaluate the potential impact of each type of emergency. Human impact should reflect the possibility of death or injury including key management and response personnel. As to property, the numbers should reflect property damage and losses, including replacement cost, temporary replacement cost, and cost of repair. Business impact should reflect potential loss of market share and dollars, including: business interruptions, employee absenteeism, breach of supply contracts, imposition of fines, penalties, and legal costs; interruption of critical supplies, and product distribution. Environmental impact should reflect the possibility and severity of contamination, and an estimate of all resulting legal, response, and remediation costs.

The internal and external resources columns should reflect a company's ability to respond to the designated emergencies. Each emergency should be evaluated, from beginning to end, considering all resources that the company would need for a proper response. If the team identifies gaps, responses could include:

- Developing additional emergency procedures
- Conducting additional training
- Acquiring additional equipment
- Establishing mutual aid agreements
- Drafting agreements with specialized contractors
- Stockpiling emergency equipment

After completing this evaluation, the numbers in each row should be added and tallied to the right. The lower the score the better. This quantitative risk assessment will help determine planning and resource priorities for use in the development or modification of an emergency response plan.

3.   The Response Plan

a.   Basic Components

The response plan should contain an executive summary stating a brief overview of the following:

- The purpose of the plan
- The facility's emergency management policy
- Authorities and responsibilities of key personnel
- The types of emergencies that could occur
- The location of a response operations command center

Next, an emergency management section should briefly describe the facility's emergency response procedures. Whenever possible, these procedures should be developed as a series of checklists that can be quickly assessed. Core elements include:

122

- Direction and control
- Communications
- Life safety
- Property protection
- Environmental protection

- Community outreach
- Recovery and restoration
- Administration and logistics

The primary <u>assessment and protective procedures</u> should focus on the first three days following an emergency. Secondary procedures should focus on getting the business back up and running. Specific procedures should be established for particular events, such as earthquakes, toxic releases and floods. All of the following should be addressed:

- Warning employees
- Communicating with responders
- Conducting an evacuation
- Accounting for all personnel
- Managing response activities

- Maintaining an operations center
- Fighting fires
- Shutting down operations
- Protecting vital records
- Restoring operations

Finally, the plan needs to attach key <u>support documents</u>. Call lists should set forth the names, responsibilities, and 24-hour telephone numbers of on and off-site personnel who would respond to an emergency. Mutual aid agreements should be referenced, or attached, as well as building and site maps, showing the following:

- Utility shutoffs
- Water hydrants
- Water main valves
- Water lines
- Gas main valves
- Gas lines
- Hazardous materials
- Electrical cutoffs
- Electrical substations
- Storm drains
- Sewer lines

- Precise location of each building
- Floor plans
- Alarms
- Fire extinguishers
- Fire suppression systems
- Exits
- Stairways
- Designated escape routes
- Restricted areas
- High-value items

b.   Media Relations

Proper planning includes saying the right thing in an emergency. If someone mishandles the news of an emergency, it can harm the community, employees, and the company. The principles and techniques for effective public relations and public affairs management are constant. Whether prompted by plant disaster, environmental threat, lawsuit, or regulatory ban, a company should respond with a well-thought plan, including:

- Pre-crisis distribution of media relations plan to all employees [309]
- Management should designate one senior person to speak[310]
- Key operating personnel, e.g., plant managers, should remain accessible[311]
- Background/crisis information should be released as soon as possible[312]

---

[309] Despite whom is designated as an information source, the press may approach any employee with questions. Reporters may question the office professional who answers the phone, the guard at the plant gate or workers as they leave the facility.

[310] A centralized information source can provide reliable information to the media in an orderly way. When an emergency arises, news people want to know the facts immediately. Newspapers, radio and television stations monitor police scanners for police, fire, and for rescue equipment dispatches. Photographers and reporters hurry to the scene with cameras and recorders, demanding access to the area. If a company seems secretive, disorganized, or deceptive, it can sustain permanent damage to its image.

[311] In emergencies, confusion is likely and rumors proliferate. People may make conflicting and exaggerated statements. A person in authority can help restore calm and reinforce the reliability of what the spokesperson has already said.

[312] The Ford Motor Company advises in its Crisis Communications Plan, "Gather the facts, disclose them promptly and tell the truth. There must be a sense of urgency." Reporters will want to know the history of the company, who owns it, facts about the facility or equipment involved, and biographical information about the people the crisis affects. Product literature is often helpful, especially photographs of plants.

- Lists of people/agencies that need to be notified should be kept on file[313]
- Advise stakeholders (e.g., customers/shareholders) of impacts

c.   Personnel Considerations

Most managers know little about supervising someone affected by traumatic stress. A recurrent issue after the Northridge earthquake was the perception of insensitive supervisors who exacerbated employees' trauma.

A comprehensive emergency preparedness process should train managers to recognize and handle traumatic stress, including knowing when to request intervention resources. Effective performance of employees during and after a disaster requires special considerations, including:

- Provisions for emergency food, water, and housing for critical workers[314]
- Anticipation of transportation problems[315]
- Realization that personal priorities change during a crisis[316]
- Training emergency response employees in advance

---

[313] The media represent the community at large, but inform employees directly. If the event injures people, reach families immediately by telephone or in person. Depending on the type of emergency, governmental agencies and other groups may also need notification.

[314] Restaurants and hotels may not be in operation after a disaster because water, gas, and electric service may not be available.

[315] Transportation delays after a natural disaster may hinder the emergency response and recovery employees' travel to and from work. Alternative work locations and telecommuting should be considered where feasible. Additionally, on-site traffic-flow patterns and site security may be modified to facilitate personnel access.

[316] A good way to prepare for changes in priorities is to hold some resources in reserve, including human resources. At the beginning of a crisis, everyone starts off with a tremendous burst of energy, but may wear out in a short time.

125

d. Finalizing the Plan

A first draft of the plan should be distributed for review and comments. As part of a second review, the team should conduct a tabletop exercise involving all key response personnel. In a conference room setting, the team describes an emergency scenario and participants discuss their responsibilities and proposed actions. The team should then modify the plan according to identified areas of confusion and overlap.

Once a final version is ready, the team should brief senior management to obtain written approval. The final plan is usually in 3-ring binders for easy updating. Everyone who receives a copy should sign for it and be responsible for posting subsequent changes. The company should distribute the approved plan to senior managers, the lead personnel on the emergency response team, company headquarters, and appropriate community emergency response agencies. Key personnel should keep a copy of the plan both at work and in their homes.

4. Implementation

Implementation involves integrating the plan into company operations, training employees, periodic evaluation, and modifications. To be effective, an emergency response plan must be part of the corporate culture. Opportunities should be taken to build awareness and train personnel involving all levels of management and community response organizations.

a. Training

Training is appropriate for anyone who works at or regularly visits the facility. The team should develop a training and drill plan. These efforts should be based on an employee's physical location within the facility and plan-identified responsibilities. To keep enthusiasm high, it is a good idea to rotate certain responsibilities yearly. Attached as Appendix "Y" is a sample *Training and Drill Exercises Worksheet* that a company should tailor to its specific response needs.

The team should regularly schedule orientation and education sessions to provide information, answer questions, and identify needs and concerns. Tabletop exercises should continue beyond plan development and into the training period. This is a cost-effective way to identify areas of overlap and confusion before conducting more demanding training activities.

126

The emergency management group and response team should conduct walk-through drills for specific functions. This activity generally involves more people and is more thorough than a tabletop exercise. Drills should focus on specific functions, such as medical response, emergency notifications, warnings and communications, and equipment. The number of functions covered by a single drill should be limited, and personnel should be encouraged to identify problem areas. For example, an evacuation drill would allow personnel to walk the evacuation route to a designated area for a "head count." The organizers should request that participants make notes as they progress through what might become a hazard during an emergency, e.g., stairways cluttered with debris or unventilated hallways. They should modify plans accordingly.

Finally, the management group should conduct a full-scale exercise simulating a real life emergency as closely as possible. This exercise should optimally involve all emergency response personnel, employees, management and community response organizations.

b.   Periodic Evaluation and Modification

The company should conduct a formal audit of the entire plan at least once a year. Whenever they contemplate a new location for any operations, the management group should complete a hazard analysis of the area. The company should also evaluate the plan after each training drill or actual emergency. Audits should address the following:

- Does it address problems identified in the vulnerability analysis?
- Do key personnel understand their responsibilities?
- Does it address facility layout or operational changes?
- Are photographs and other facility records up to date?
- Are training objectives being met?
- Are names, responsibilities and telephone numbers current?

Modifications of the plan should be common. Since businesses change, the company should not view the plan as a one-time endeavor. All good plans (whether for a game, battle, investment, advertisement or otherwise), are fluid and change as circumstances require. This point emphasizes the need to have all levels of the company involved in evaluating and modifying the plan.

B.   Case Studies

1.   Chemical Release, Union Carbide (Bhopal, India)

On the morning of December 3, 1984, news of the disaster at Bhopal swept across Europe and the world.[317] Ultimately, the deadly release of the chemical MIC (methylisocyanate) killed more than 2,000 people. Quick action and a wise "openness" philosophy prevented this terrible crisis from destroying a huge international company. Less than three months before the disaster, Union Carbide had asked a multinational European consultant to develop a general communication plan for the company. Although the plan was not complete, they had established a general framework.

That December morning, a telex reached the consultant's London office: the BBC had just announced an accident at a Union Carbide plant in India, citing the figure of twenty-five deaths. Half an hour later, a call came from the office in Stockholm: a Swedish radio crew that happened to be in Bombay was citing 200 dead. When the consultant called the Union Carbide Europe headquarters in Geneva a half hour later nobody knew about the accident. The company headquarters in Danbury, Connecticut, however, where it was 4:00 a.m., was already alerted.

By mid-morning the next day, the company had faxed a crisis plan to the Geneva offices outlining basic strategy: no comment until they named a spokesperson, except to say that they knew about the event, that they were taking steps to alleviate the suffering of the victims, and that they would provide the media information when it came in. By that evening, some reports estimated deaths at up to 400.

One immediate decision was to name four spokespersons. Language and knowledge were both problems. Two generalists were named: one vice-president, who spoke fluent English and French, and the communications consultant who spoke seven languages. For technical questions, they made available two top-notch chemists who were experts on the deadly MIC.

By the next morning, a crisis room was established in the Geneva headquarters. A chalkboard was set up listing question-responding rules:

- No contradictions among spokespersons

---

[317] This section is adapted from: Patrick Lagadec, States of Emergency, Butterworth-Heineman (1990).

128

- No questions without answers; if the answer is unknown, promise to find it and do so
- Generalists never answer a technical question
- Mandatory politeness and maximum patience in all contacts

Externally, the company first sent a telex to some 800 European media stating that they would respond to all inquires. The company set up a logbook and recorded each telex, each telephone call, each request, and each interview. A chemist and an executive secretary worked on the logging effort full time. This 300-page document helped track the information effort for two years and allowed the company to evaluate the mistakes made. To guarantee a perfect coherency between Geneva and Zurich, they established an open telephone line between the two sites (i.e., they never hung up the receiver). In the first few hours, 40% of the calls were from the different Union Carbide Europe subsidiaries; 40% from the media; 10% from industries and governments; and 10% were from public relations agencies offering their services.

Internally, a priority was to inform Union Carbide's employees. Twice a day an "internal information report" was posted in company cafeterias updating the situation. This is a vital lesson: priorities should include informing the company's own employees (to help calm people and stop the rumor mill). The company ultimately completed an informational video for its 7,200 employees in Europe.

During the second week following the accident, a special informational conference was held during a meeting of the European chemical industry. With Union Carbide putting all its cards on the table, the exchange with the competitors went much better than expected. The company also conducted a European tour every two or three weeks, visiting the major capitals and distributing the latest available information.

The CEO himself took time to become personally involved, both in the United States and abroad. He was there in person, not to defend himself or make excuses, but to explain what had happened and to guarantee that the company would take moral responsibility for this catastrophe. Some people raised legal arguments about keeping admissions to a minimum. However, the company finally decided that Union Carbide should admit to its mistakes. The company (and its stock) ultimately rebounded, having learned that communication is not always just a matter of technology and professionalism, but a question of corporate culture and philosophy.

2.   Fires

a.   Overview

In 1993, property losses from fires within the United States exceeded $8.5 billion.[318] In the industrial and manufacturing facility category, metal and metal products manufacturers had the highest losses, with 21% of the fires and 11% of the property damage in that category.[319]

The following are select examples showing the dynamics of industrial explosions/fires:

• On April 6, 1995, a two million square foot steel mill in West Virginia caught fire. The cause was a hydraulic oil mist spray igniting upon contact with an electric space heater. The owners had equipped the plant with eleven separate sprinkler systems, and its own fire department. The blaze set off one sprinkler system with 250 sprinklers, which shut down quickly when the fire burned through the secondary power cables for the electric fire pumps. After four hours of burning, the fire caused $75,000,000 in property damage and injured seventeen employees.[320]

• On May 27, 1994, a runaway reaction in an Ohio chemical facility caused an explosion of ignited flammable liquids stored in a tank farm. The plant had no emergency detection or suppression systems. Three employees died.[321]

• On April 20, 1994, an explosion of unknown origin killed four

_____

[318] S. Badger and F. Fahy, "Billion-Dollar Drop in Large-Loss Property Fire," National Fire Protection Association Journal, (November/December, 1995).

[319] S. Swartrout and P. Moore, "Planning for Recovery in a Manufacturing Environment," Disaster Recovery Journal, (January, February, March, 1995).

[320] "Billion-Dollar Drop in Large-Loss Property Fire," supra.

[321] K. Tremblay, "Catastrophic Fires of 1994," National Fire Protection Association Journal, (September/October, 1995).

employees at a steel manufacturing plant. Four fire fighters were injured, three from exposure to a phosphoric acid solution. The facility had no emergency detection or suppression systems.[322]

At least three lessons are evident from the above incidents: 1) prevent fires and explosions from occurring; 2) have fire detection and suppression systems in place; and 3) be sure the detection suppression system will operate properly during an emergency.

b.   Office Fires

Within seven minutes after a fire ignited in a wastebasket containing typical office trash, flashover occurred and near-ceiling gas temperatures reached at least 1,600° F.[323] About 90 seconds later, flames filled the entire room and eventually consumed all of its combustible furnishings. This fire test, conducted by Factory Mutual Engineering and Research (FME&R), erases the notion that offices have low fire risks. Another FME&R study of 490 office building fires calculated the average loss at $260,000.

The following examples offer chilling evidence of the fire hazards inherent in the average office environment:

- On February 23, 1991, a twelve-alarm fire burned for nineteen hours, killing three fire fighters and gutting eight floors of One Meridian Plaza in Philadelphia.

- On May 4, 1988, a blaze killed one person and destroyed four floors of the sixty-two story First Interstate Bank in Los Angeles. Sixty-four fire companies battled the fire for three-and-one-half hours before bringing it under control.

- On June 30, 1989, Atlanta's Peachtree 25th Building fire killed five people, injured twenty others, and heavily damaged the floor on

---

[322] Id.

[323] Adapted from: "Taking Steps to Decrease the Risk of Office Fires," Factory Mutual Engineering and Research, Disaster Recovery World, Vol. II, presented by the Disaster Recovery Journal.

which the blaze originated.

c.   Fire Prevention

Properly installed sprinkler systems, and other basic protection equipment can greatly reduce the chance of significant losses from fire. Fire prevention, however, is more than a matter of simply installing hardware. The best way to safeguard against fire loss is to assure that fires do not start.

Various defects in electrical wiring or the improper and careless use of electrical equipment were the probable cause of 30% of the office fires from 1985 to 1989. Professional testing maintenance is the key to reducing this risk. Another effective way to safeguard against fires is to reduce the number of combustible materials. Consider using metal furniture (particularly wastebaskets) and limiting the availability of upholstered furniture. Instruct employees to store combustibles inside fire-safe desks and cabinets when possible.

Renovations may cause the shut-off of fire protection systems or water-control valves. Paints, cleaning solvents and other highly combustible materials are often present during renovations without adequate storage or ventilation. In addition, dangerous, portable open-flame equipment, such as torches and space heaters, may be used. During renovations, owners should install automatic sprinklers, if not already present. Managers must also take steps to assure that the work environment will be safe after the renovation. For instance, when having suspended ceilings installed, be sure to provide sprinkler protection above and below the ceiling. This tip is especially important when the roof or floor deck above is combustible (as in low-rise office buildings) or the space can sustain a spreading fire.

3.   Floods

During the past decade, U.S. floods accounted for several hundred million dollars in industrial property damage.[324] While these figures are staggering, even more disturbing is the fact that such losses could have been averted or reduced with prudent flood protection measures.

---

[324] Adapted from: "Surviving the Deluge," Factory Mutual Engineering and Research, Disaster Recovery World, Vol. II (1995).

a.   Risk Evaluation

The first step is determining whether a facility is at risk from flooding. Ideally, this occurs before site selection. Owners can attain necessary information from U.S. Army Corps of Engineers reports, and flood maps from the Federal Insurance Administration (FIA), and the U.S. Geological Survey. Maps and other resources from these sources show flood plains and potential flood severity. "Flood zones" lie within a larger area called a "flood plain," which is a low-lying land area next to a body of water that either has flooded or could possibly flood. Flood severity is reflected by recurrence intervals, e.g., 10-year, 50-year, 100-year and 500-year floods. The greater the time, the greater the severity of the flood.

If a facility is considered at risk from flooding, the company must make a thorough inventory of material assets and assess potential losses. Equipment, storage, and the building itself may be soaked, and subject to further damage from water flow. The aftermath is no better: heavy deposits of silt and debris may be left behind, making cleanup and salvage a slow, expensive process.

b.   Preparation and Recovery

There are three types of flood protection. First, permanent flood protection is always in place, and requires little or no human action to be effective. Experts consider flood walls and dikes the most effective, and expensive, forms of permanent protection where property and equipment values are extremely high and the possibility of salvage is low. However, flood damage potential may justify a flood wall or dike to protect the facility. Sometimes the cost can be prohibitive for one company to build its own wall, but cooperation among several neighboring companies can make the project feasible. Additional, less expensive permanent flood protection measures include:

- Bricking up ground-level windows (only halfway if low-level flooding is expected)
- Installing flood doors suspended by pulleys/counterweights or mounted on rails
- Installing hand-operated valves to prevent backflow through floor drains or plumbing fixtures
- Building flood walls around vital equipment such as furnaces,

computers, and switchgear

Second, <u>contingent flood protection</u> is not permanently installed. This level of protection is advisable if facilities are in a geographical area where authorities can provide warning before a flood. Flood shields are the most common form of contingent protection. Contractors can quickly bolt these shields onto door and window frames. They should number the shields to match their corresponding doors or windows to prevent last-minute confusion. If flood shields are chosen as a form of contingent protection, it is extremely important that they cover all openings, since one missed opening could jeopardize an otherwise well-protected facility.

Third, <u>emergency flood protection</u> requires relatively quick action. Typical methods include:

- Sandbagging possible flood entry points
- Moving high-value or critical items to higher stories or safer buildings
- Covering machines with water displacing compounds, or plastic sheets
- Filling empty storage tanks to prevent their floating

Emergency protection requires that trained employees be on call. The best way to achieve this mobilization of labor is through the formation of an on-site Emergency Organization ("E.O."), consisting of employees who reside outside the flood-prone area. As few as one quarter of the work force may be available in a flood emergency. Those who reside in the flood-prone area will understandably turn their attention to protecting their own homes and families. Therefore, selecting E.O. members who will be available both mentally and physically is best.

Duties for members of the E.O. should include such activities as filling and placing sandbags, securing flood shields, and moving equipment and stock. In addition, they should outline salvage priorities, starting with those items requiring immediate care. One of the greatest problems after a natural disaster is overcoming a negative attitude. The company should train E.O. members in salvage techniques. What looks like a total loss may be recoverable, if a comprehensive salvage plan is put into action immediately. Salvage plans should not rely on vulnerable services, such as electrical, water, or outside contractors, that may not be available during a flood.

A well-designed flood protection program should also compliment the existing fire prevention plan, since flood waters often carry heavy debris that can ram

134

and rupture flammable liquid tanks or piping. Water can carry these liquids to an ignition source. If sprinkler piping or the fire pumps have suffered damage and flood waters cut off the facility from the fire department, a fire could burn out of control. The danger of fire also increases after flood waters recede. A flood cleanup may generate large piles of combustible materials at a facility, and any cutting or welding done during salvage will increase the risk of fire. Therefore, delaying cutting and welding is advisable until sprinkler systems are back in service, combustibles are removed, and a fire watch is established.

c.   Monsanto, 1993 Mississippi Flood (St. Louis, Missouri)

Monsanto employs about 250 people at its household item manufacturing plant in south St. Louis, Missouri.[325] The Mississippi River Valley flood in the summer of 1993 affected industry along thousands of miles through many states. Monsanto closely watched the water level as of July 6, stopped all plant operations on July 9. Shortly thereafter, plant employees began building a dike to protect buildings and key manufacturing areas. A host of volunteers soon joined plant employees from other Monsanto locations in the St. Louis area. Together, everyone worked around the clock to construct a 50,000 sandbag wall (1,200 feet long and up to 10 feet high).

On July 11, the wall between the plant and the river was complete. Monsanto constructed the dike to withstand a crest of 47 feet, which was two feet higher than the Army Corps of Engineers's initial 45-foot projection. However, when the wall was completed, the Corps increased the crest prediction to 46 feet and then 47 feet. Monsanto officials set themselves up for problems by not planning sufficiently beyond the initial projections, i.e., for a worst case scenario.

Flood experts and prior victims gave Monsanto advice, including:

•   Identify and block all possible water inlets into the plant, including sewers

---

[325] Adapted from: Eric Brimer, P.E. and Thomas Hinrichs, "Prepare for the Worst and Hope for the Best," <u>Natural Disaster Experiences,</u> American Academy of Environmental Engineers (1995).

135

- Get portable equipment (e.g., pumps/electric generators)
- Monitor utility systems that run throughout the infrastructure
- Change traffic-flow patterns and modify site security

Since Monsanto did not have a flood preparedness plan in place, it developed a clear emergency mission: to "safely, and without environmental impact, reduce the effect of the flood on the plant, the customers, and the business." They decided to handle the flood like any other plant emergency, using the plant's normal "incident command process." The most important element was establishing a "RACI" approach (be "Responsible and Accountable, Consult, and Inform").

Monsanto set up a command center, which became the main hub for the plant's flood response efforts. Information flowed into and out of the plant, the Army Corp. of Engineers, local emergency agencies, and other Monsanto offices. All of the plant's day-shift workers attended daily meetings to learn news about the river and response activities. The most serious communications breakdown flowed from the Corps of Engineers' projected crest readings. They projected crest readings for the Eads Bridge in downtown St. Louis, while the Monsanto plant sits several miles south on the River Des Peres. Since the river's elevation declines all the way to the Gulf of Mexico, the projected downtown crest reading was inaccurate at the plant. The experience revealed that engineers, first responders, management information systems personnel, manufacturers, and federal agencies do not use a common language.

Monsanto also formed multi-functional, multi-level teams to plan and carry out key activities. The teams had to undertake a range of tasks simultaneously, including:

- Immediate flood prevention
- Interim plant operations[326]
- Cleanup and decontamination after the flood

The company installed pumps to keep the plant dry from seepage and rainfall. Monsanto moved key electrical equipment including the phone system, two

---

[326] The multiple tasks required to maintain interim plant operations during high water included: securing the utilities and raw materials needed to resume operation, starting an interim wastewater handling system, providing temporary office and laboratory facilities, and training people to operate new facilities.

motor control centers and switch gear for one manufacturing unit and one packaging unit to higher elevation. This was done to allow a quick startup in the event the levee breached, and to permit manufacturing operations to continue in the future if faced with another high-water situation.

Monsanto survived the crest in relatively good shape. Department 20, which produces leaveners for the baking industry, had five feet of sewage covering all of its equipment in the basement, but restarted on August 17, just ten days after returning to the plant. Its initial operations were at a full rate with no "off-spec" product generated in the process. The day before Department 20 returned to operation, the U.S. Food and Drug Administration conducted an unannounced inspection. The plant passed.

Besides returning the plant to operation, several other goals were achieved during the crisis:

- No employee injuries, despite heavy lifting in high heat and humidity
- No loss of customers
- Management gave support throughout the crisis
- Plant staff remained employed
- No detectable community resentment

In hindsight, Monsanto agreed that it should have devoted more time to defining responsibilities. Any time spent clarifying roles, setting expectations, gaining understanding, and obtaining commitment, would have quickly been recovered.

4.   Earthquakes

a.   Special Risks

Earthquake risk is a reality throughout the world. The necessity for earthquake preparedness relates directly to potential seismic activity and vulnerability of operations. Authorities record one million earthquakes each year worldwide, with more than 600 causing damage to building structures.[327]

---

[327] R. Flint and B. Skinner, Physical Geology, 2nd. Ed., John Wiley & Sons, p. 396-7 (1977).

The Atlantic Ocean is widening at a rate of five centimeters per year,[328] with the North American Continent moving an average of two centimeters per year.[329] Experts believe that in the U.S. only southern Florida, southern Texas, and parts of Alabama and Mississippi are earthquake risk-free.[330] By contrast, substantial areas in each of the following states are at major risk of damage from seismic activity: New York,[331] Illinois, Indiana, Kentucky, Tennessee/Missouri,[332] South Carolina, Arkansas, Montana, Idaho, Utah, Arizona, Washington and California.[333]

The January 17, 1994 Northridge earthquake, resulting in fifty-seven dead, nearly 10,000 injured and more than $20 billion in property damage, occurred on a previously unknown fault below the San Fernando Valley.[334] Similarly, on January 17, 1995, the Kobe earthquake killed 5,100 people, injured 27,000 more, and caused property damage (reconstruction costs) of $64.2 billion. There had been no earthquake in the Kobe region for 79 years,[335] and no major earthquake (magnitude 7.0 or greater) for more than 1,000 years.[336]

---

[328] D. Ballantyne, P.E., "Reevaluating System Vulnerability after an Earthquake," Natural Disaster Experiences, American Academy of Environmental Engineers (1995).

[329] Flint and Skinner, Physical Geology, supra.

[330] Id.

[331] New York City recently adopted the first seismic building codes in its history. "Eastern Quake's Costs and Damages could Eclipse Northridge," Civil Engineering (November, 1995).

[332] The New Madrid Fault Zone includes both Memphis, Tennessee, and St. Louis, Missouri.

[333] Flint and Skinner, Physical Geology, supra.

[334] "The Northridge earthquake, January 17, 1994," Dames & Moore (1995).

[335] "Quake Preparedness is a Japanese Obsession," The Orange County Register, News p. 26 (February 12, 1995).

[336] "Event Report: Japan-The Great Hanshin Earthquake, January 17, 1995," supra.

Conducting an earthquake vulnerability evaluation on a structure or system typically improves preparedness not only for the subject of the evaluation, but for multiple other components of a facility. With each evaluation, engineers improve their understanding of earthquake loading and structural and system responses to those loads. This evaluation typically includes five elements:

- Definition of post-earthquake operating objectives
- Evaluation of earthquake hazards and the extent of expected damage
- Assessment of the performance of individual system components
- Assessment of overall system performance
- Development and implementation of mitigation programs

Earthquake hazards fall into two categories: ground shaking and permanent ground deformation (PGD). Experts further categorize PGD as tectonic deformation (including fault movement or regional tectonic cracking) and/or soil failure (such as liquefaction/lateral spread and landslide caused by ground shaking).[337] Above-grade structures are more vulnerable to shaking. Below-grade structures, such as pipelines, are more vulnerable to PGD.

Richter magnitude and modified Mercalli intensity are more widely understood earthquake parameters than PGD. Nonprofessionals can think of Richter magnitude as the size of a bomb explosion and the modified Mercalli intensity as the effect of the explosion, considering both the size and proximity to the bomb.

Peak ground acceleration ("PGA") is often used as a measure of ground shaking, expressed as a percent of gravity ("percent g"). The Northridge earthquake produced some PGA's approaching 200 percent g. PGA's of 60 to 80 percent g were common, and considered very high.

Liquefaction may occur where poorly consolidated, sandy alluvial deposits or fills consolidate from earthquake shaking.[338] When this occurs underwater (e.g., in a high groundwater table), the consolidation results in displacement of water that tries to escape, liquefying the sand into a quick condition. On a

---

[337] "Reevaluating System Vulnerability After An Earthquake," supra.

[338] Liquefaction was widespread in the Marina District of San Francisco, causing extensive damage, during the 1989 Loma Prieta earthquake.

significant grade, or there is a free face nearby, the soil mass can move laterally.

b.   System Performance

Almost by definition, one key consideration in earthquake engineering is interdependence of system components. The vulnerability of tanks, utilities, and key operational systems is quantified using a combination of empirical damage information and structural analysis. Planners can rate plant vulnerability as the expected downtime. They might define ranges of damage as follows:

Mitigation Priority	Expected Damage/Downtime
1	Heavy = nonfunctional, long-term outage
2	Moderate = nonfunctional, three days repair
3	Light = still operable
4	No damage

They must also assess the importance of system components to the functioning of the system. One approach is to quantify components' importance using the following rating system:

Mitigation Priority	Importance to System
1	Crucial - only component providing service
2	Important - system operates at 70% if component is down
3	Would slightly impair service
4	Component not required

By combining the vulnerability of system components and their importance to the system's functioning, planners may rank any required earthquake mitigation.

No widely adopted guidelines or standards are available regarding the expected performance of industrial facilities following an earthquake. The building industry has defined earthquake performance objectives as follows: professionals should design buildings not to collapse in a major earthquake, allowing occupants to evacuate, and to sustain only minor, repairable structural damage in a moderate earthquake.

c.   Storage Tanks and Pipelines

Older steel tanks that were not seismically-designed and constructed can suffer buckling at the bottom (elephants' foot bulge) and in their shells and roofs.[339] Companies should seismically retrofit these older tanks. Sloshing in large storage tanks can cause damage, leading to the malfunction of other equipment as well. Methods to abate sloshing should be considered in the design of mechanical equipment and baffles for large tanks.

Above-ground storage tanks have the poorest track record of surviving disasters, particularly earthquakes. These tanks tend to fail in elephants' foot buckling, or in less severe cases, break connecting piping. Often, connecting piping fails because of the differential movement between the tank and the piping. Companies should employ methods to provide a more flexible connection between the tank and the piping that can withstand differential movement.

d.   Mitigation Programs

An earthquake evaluation will have little significance if it does not lead to mitigation measures. Earthquake mitigation programs should identify an initial phase of low-cost steps, followed by steps that the owners can carry out in the medium- and long-term, by integration into the facility's capital improvement plans.

Low-cost mitigation measures can include developing and setting up standards, emergency planning, and equipment anchoring. Vulnerable facility components that may pose a threat to life, such as hazardous chemical systems and at-risk buildings, should also be upgraded in the initial phase. Medium- and long-term mitigation steps requiring more capital include general tank and building upgrades, and replacing pipeline and storage tanks.

e.   Nissan Emergency Response Plan (Carson, California)

Nissan Motor Corporation, USA has more than 1,100 employees at its corporate headquarters in Southern California (city of Carson). Its facilities

---

[339] Id.

consist of eight buildings with more than 600,000 square feet. Before drafting its current emergency response plan, Nissan hired a disaster response consultant. His risk analysis showed that the facilities were subject to: earthquakes, toxic clouds from several nearby chemical and refinery plants, explosions or releases from underground pipelines next to the facilities, and hazardous material incidents from three major freeways nearby. Of the potential threats, a high magnitude earthquake on the Inglewood-Newport fault (approximately 2.5 miles away) represented the greatest danger.

Nissan developed an emergency response plan based on the worst-case earthquake scenario (magnitude seven or higher). The plan was developed to apply to multiple catastrophic events. The scenario presumed severe conditions for 72 hours following the event, including: no outside help, loss of electricity (except emergency power) and phones, elevators out-of-service with employees still in them, and potential fires, injuries, and structural damage.

Nissan concluded that each floor of its multiple offices may have to survive for a period on its own. Thus, instead of a centralized response approach, the company went with a decentralized Response Team for each floor or main section of a building. The size of the team varied with the number of people on the floor. All team members were volunteers without regard to position in the company, although managers were encouraged to participate.

The company began to carry out the plan through a two-day training program. The training included CPR, first aid, team leadership in disasters, fire fighting (use of extinguishers), smoke room experience, and rescues. While the two-day training period required significant compression of activities, Nissan thought that three or more days would have resulted in a significant reduction in volunteers' and management's willingness to release employees from work. The drill emphasized experienced trainers and hands-on practice. They used "Hollywood style" makeup to simulate injuries and purchased a smoke generator for rescues in smoke-filled rooms. Class size was kept at 12 or less with lunch provided.

Volunteers appeared to leave self-confident, enthusiastic, feeling good about their team, and with a CPR card valid for two years. Nissan trained more than 160 people as response team members. Additionally, special food, water, medical and emergency supplies were placed on each floor. Two-way radios were installed on each floor to allow communication between floors and with company emergency operations command centers. Subsequent employee mailings (every six months) stressed personal responsibility to be prepared at home, at work, and in cars, advertising survival kits at reduced prices. Continued preparedness plans include monthly refresher training, alternating between two-hour formal training and one-hour informal training; once a year, the local Fire Department helps carry out a formal exercise.

f.   Rocketdyne, 1994 Northridge Quake
(Canoga Park, California)

On January 17, 1994, when the Northridge earthquake rumbled through Southern California, companies had the chance to implement their contingency plans.[340] No matter how well prepared they thought they were, many were greatly disappointed. No one predicted the amount of structural damage that occurred. Buildings that contractors built "up to code" were no longer habitable and freeways supposed to withstand earthquakes of much greater magnitudes, buckled and collapsed under the intense shaking.

The Rocketdyne Division of Rockwell International is located in Canoga Park, just two miles from the quake's epicenter. It sustained major damage. Three computer labs supporting the space station program received the brunt of the damage. More than 70 pieces of computer equipment were involved from desktop computers, modems, printers and other miscellaneous peripherals to Digital Equipment Corporation VAX mainframes.

At daybreak, Ken Tcheng, manager of technical management information systems and his staff ventured to Rocketdyne to assess damage. Not sure if the building was safe, they slowly made their way in to find that the quake had caused a water pipe to burst on the floor above the computer labs. Knowing they did not have much time before leaving the premises, they quickly shut the computer system down and cut the circuit breakers to prevent any power surges when they restored electricity.

Rocketdyne had to wait for three days and many aftershocks until the building inspectors deemed the building safe. When staff finally entered, they discovered an even bigger mess. The upper floors flooded the room with water and moisture and dust was in the air. To top it off, both the shaking and the weight of the water above had caused the ceiling tiles to fall.

---

[340] Adapted from: Mark Fritz, "Recovery Planning Proves Effective During an Earthquake," Disaster Recovery Journal, (April, May, June 1994).

The company quickly contacted the VAX vendor to assess the system. Before even beginning to look at the equipment, the local restoration team advised Rocketdyne to turn on the heating system and/or dehumidifiers to help stop any further corrosion. They wanted to control the environment as soon as possible. That meant starting with temperature and humidity. It also meant disposing of any standing water and moisture on the walls, and throwing out all the damaged ceiling tiles.

The vendor presented Rocketdyne with a complete restoration plan that included disassembling the computers, peripherals and all other electronic equipment, restoration and decontamination, and reassembly. Everything in the computer lab had to be recovered due to moisture damage. The entire job was estimated to take three days. Once debris was removed and moisture controlled, the next step was to tackle the equipment. Fifteen restoration specialists from all over the country worked hand-in-hand with VAX technicians and Rocketdyne engineers. In two days, the restoration part of the recovery was done. The VAX systems were brought back on-line, prepared for some system failures. The computers operated flawlessly, however. No data had been lost.

Tcheng explains that Rocketdyne has been working on a new disaster plan. "As you can imagine this was all new to us. No one ever expected an earthquake of this magnitude nor the type of damage we had. We learned a lot. We now have a much better idea of what to do if this or any other major catastrophe happens. We knew enough to cut the power. Now we know how to help prevent further contamination while we are waiting for the professionals to start the recovery process."

CHAPTER 12
REFERENCE SOURCES

The following sections provide several sources of reference materials relating to this book, the environment, and the precious metals industry.

A.   Appendices on Computer Disk

The appendices are contained on a 3½ inch computer disk attached to the back cover. Instructions and other technical information appear as the computer file "help" on the disk. This ready-to-use-and-print approach is helpful with forms such as the IPMI Membership Application and the various checklists and worksheets.

B.   IPMI Library

The Chemist's Club Library maintains the IPMI library at 40 West 45th Street, New York, NY 10036. Phone: 212/626-9203. Fax: 212/626-9379.

C.   Internet Sites (Environmental/Precious Metals Industry)

While doing research for this book, the velocity at which computers shrink the world continued to impress the author. For example, in mere minutes on the Internet, he "visited" precious metals industry home pages across the globe, including:

*   New York Mercantile Exchange[341]
*   Royal Canadian Mint[342]
*   Johnson Matthey (England)[343]
*   Trelleborg Group (Sweden)[344]

---

[341]   http://www.ino.com/gen/nymex/whatsnew.html

[342]   http://www.rcmint.ca/cgi-bin/imagemap/rcm.map?41,20

[343]   http://www.eznet.com/jme/jmhp.htm

[344]   http://www.trellgroup.se/trellgroup/

- Chugoku Kogyo (Japan)[345]

The Internet is a global network of computers that allow access to information stored at host computer "servers" around the world.[346] The Internet began as a project of the U.S. Pentagon's Advanced Research Projects Agency, designed to send packets of information from one supercomputer to another over high speed transmission lines without a predetermined course. Computer pioneers had the first four systems in place in 1969, reaching thirty-seven by 1972. In the 1980's the Internet began to really grow, mainly at universities. By 1989, the number of Internet hosts surpassed 100,000.

In the 1990's, new network technologies emerged which fostered the birth of the World Wide Web (a "hypermedia" retrieval system). Hypermedia is any medium that links to an image, sound, animation, or video file. The type of information on the Web varies widely, with documents on every imaginable subject. Web "browsers" allow the user to search for information by subject, title, name, or concept. The Web is now the fastest growing segment of the Internet. At the beginning of 1993, there were approximately one million Web sites; by July 1995, there were nearly seven million!

The volume of environmental and/or precious metals-related information on the Internet is increasing daily. In fact, many Internet sites visited were still "under construction" (i.e., they are adding more material). To provide some guidance to Web sites that might be of interest to the environmental and/or precious metals community, the author compiled the *Internet Addresses: Environmental/Precious Metals List*, attached as Appendix "Z."

This directory is only a sampling of the sites that might be of interest. Please use "browsers" (e.g., Netscape or Microsoft Explorer) to get the latest information. This voyage may include finding IPMI member companies that have home pages the author did not visit or which have come on-line since he submitted the final version of this book for printing.

---

[345] http://www.chemical-metal.co.jp/cgk/cm.html

[346] Adapted from: Briggs-Erickson, Environmental Guide to the Internet (2nd Ed., 1996).

APPENDICES

A   IPMI International Membership (List)
B   IPMI Membership Application (Form)
C   Biennial Waste Report (Form)
D   NCP Compliance (Checklist)
E   Preliminary Environmental Audit (Form)
F   Master Consulting Agreement (Example)
G   Phase I Consultant Selection (Checklist)
H   Assessing Current Facility Operations (Checklist)
I   Facility Information (Worksheet)
J   Characterizing Individual Waste Streams (Worksheet)
K   Description of Input Materials (Worksheet)
L   Options for Minimizing Hazardous Waste (Worksheet)
M   Specific Waste Minimization Option (Worksheet)
N   Feasibility (Worksheets)
O   Cost Estimation (Worksheets)
P   C.F.R. Hazardous Materials (Table)
Q   Hazardous Warning Label (Examples)
R   Transportation Scenarios, Precious Metals (Example)
S   Notification of Regulated Waste Activity (Form)
T   Uniform Hazardous Waste Manifest (Form)
U   Disaster Recovery Consultants (List)
V   Planning Scenario, Newport-Inglewood Fault (Summary)
W   Federal and State Emergency Management Agencies (List)
X   Vulnerability Analysis (Worksheet)
Y   Training and Drill Exercises (Worksheet)
Z   Internet Addresses: Environmental/Precious Metals (List)

IPMI INTERNATIONAL MEMBERSHIP LIST

IPMI International Membership
(as of 1/3/96)

Africa	1	Korea	3
Argentina	2	Malaysia	1
Australia	9	Netherlands	2
Belgium	8	New Zealand	3
Bermuda	1	Norway	1
Brazil	2	Peru	1
Burundi	1	Poland	4
Canada	47	Portugal	1
Chile	3	Russia	3
China	6	Saudi Arabia	1
Colombia	2	South Africa	12
Czechian Rep	1	Spain	6
Ecuador	1	Sweden	3
England	33	Switzerland	7
Estonia	1	Taiwan, ROC	3
France	5	Thailand	1
Germany	15	Turkey	1
Holland	2	UAE	1
Hong Kong	2	Ukraine	1
India	3	USSR	1
Ireland	2	Uzbekistan	1
Israel	5	W. Australia	1
Italy	6	West Germany	2
Japan	15	Yugoslavia	1
Kazakhstan	1		
		Total	235
		United States	635
		Grand Total	**870**

Appendix A

IPMI MEMBERSHIP APPLICATION FORM

MEMBERSHIPS
There are two basic types of memberships available: one to companies and the other to individuals. Memberships are computed from July 1 to June 30, IPMI's fiscal year.

Five categories are available under the company-type membership which are as follows:

	COMPANY	ANNUAL FEE:
☐	Patron*	$2000 or more
☐	Sustaining*	$750 to $2000
☐	Professional Association or Trade Organization	$500
☐	Non-Profit Institutes	$150
☐	Universities	$ 75

*These categories obtain numerous corporate benefits not available to other member categories.

	INDIVIDUALS	ANNUAL FEE:
☐	Qualified Member	$90
☐	Student	$10

Please check membership category desired

Name _____

Company _____

Address _____

_____

Phone _____ Fax _____

Make check fee payable in U.S. dollars drawn on a U.S. bank to IPMI or use ☐ Visa ☐ MasterCard ☐ American Express

☐ ☐ ☐ ☐ ■ ☐ ☐ ☐ ■ ☐ ☐ ☐ ☐ ☐

Expiration Date ☐ ☐ ☐ ☐

Mail or Fax to: IPMI, 4905 West Tilghman St., Suite 160
Allentown, PA 18104-9137 Phone 610-395-9700 Fax 610-395-5855

Appendix B

BIENNIAL WASTE REPORT FORM (1 of 2)

OMB#: 2050-0024 Expires 8/31/96

BEFORE COPYING FORM, ATTACH SITE IDENTIFICATION LABEL OR ENTER:

SITE NAME: _____

EPA ID NO: |__|__|__| |__|__|__| |__|__|__| |__|__|

U.S. ENVIRONMENTAL PROTECTION AGENCY

1995 Hazardous Waste Report

FORM
IC

IDENTIFICATION AND CERTIFICATION

INSTRUCTIONS: Read the detailed instructions beginning on page 9 of the 1995 Hazardous Waste Report booklet before completing this form.

Sec. I Site name and location address. Complete A through H. Check the box ☐ in items A, C, E, F, G, and H if same as label; if different, enter corrections. If label is absent, enter information. Instruction page 10.

A. EPA ID No. Same as label ☐ or → |__|__|__| |__|__|__| |__|__|__| |__|__|	B. County
C. Site/company name Same as label ☐ or →	D. Has the site name associated with this EPA ID changed since 1993? ☐ 1 Yes ☐ 2 No

E. Street name and number. If not applicable, enter industrial park, building name, or other physical location description.
Same as label ☐ or →

F. City, town, village, etc. Same as label ☐ or →	G. State Same as label |__|__|	H. Zip Code Same as label |__|__|__|__|__| - |__|__|__|__|

Sec. II Mailing address of site. Instruction page 10.

A. Is the mailing address the same as the location address?   ☐ 1 Yes (SKIP TO SEC. III)   ☐ 2 No (GO TO BOX B)

B. Number and street name of mailing address

C. City, town, village, etc.	D. State |__|__|	E. Zip Code |__|__|__|__|__| - |__|__|__|__|

Sec. III Name, title, and telephone number of the person who should be contacted if questions arise regarding this report. Instruction page 10.

A. Please print: Last Name First name M.I.	B. Title	C. Telephone |__|__|__| |__|__|__| - |__|__|__|__| Extension |__|__|__|__|

Sec. IV "I certify under penalty of law that this document and all attachments were prepared under my direction or supervision in accordance with a system designed to assure that qualified personnel properly gather and evaluate the information submitted. Based on my inquiry of the person or persons who manage the system, or those persons directly responsible for gathering the information, the information submitted is, to the best of my knowledge and belief, true, accurate and complete. I am aware that there are significant penalties under Section 3008 of the Resource Conservation and Recovery Act for submitting false information, including the possibility of fine and imprisonment for knowing violations."

A. Please print: Last Name First name M.I.	B. Title
C. Signature	D. Date of signature |__|__| |__|__| |__|__| MO. DAY YR.

Page 1 of ___

EPA Form 8700-13A/B (Revised (8-95)

Over →

Appendix C-1

FORM IC

EPA ID NO: |__|__|__| |__|__|__| |__|__|__| |__|__|

Sec.V - Generator Status. Instruction pages 10, 12.

A. 1995 RCRA generator status	B. Reason for not generating
(CHECK ONE BOX BELOW)	(CHECK ALL THAT APPLY)
☐ 1 LQG	☐ 1 Never generated ☐ 5 Periodic or occasional generator
☐ 2 SQG ` SKIP to SEC. VI	☐ 2 Out of business ☐ 6 Waste minimization activity
☐ 3 CESQG — ⬉	☐ 3 Only excluded or delisted waste ☐ 7 Other (SPECIFY COMMENTS IN BOX BELOW)
☐ 4 Non generator (Continue to Box B)	☐ 4 Only non-hazardous waste

---

Sec.VI - On-Site Waste Management Status. Instruction pages 13, 14.

A. Storage subject to RCRA permitting requirements	B. Treatment, disposal, or recycling subject to RCRA permitting requirements	C. RCRA-exempt treatment, disposal, or recycling

---

Sec.VII - Waste Minimization Activity during 1994 or 1995. Instruction pages 14, 15.

A. Did this site begin or expand a source reduction activity during 1994 or 1995?	B. Did this site begin or expand a recycling activity during 1994 or 1995?	C. Did this site systematically investigate opportunities for source reduction or recycling during 1994 or 1995?
☐ 1 Yes ☐ 2 No	☐ 1 Yes ☐ 2 No	☐ 1 Yes ☐ 2 No

D. Did any of the factors listed below delay or limit this site's ability to initiate new or additional source reduction activities in 1994 or 1995? (CHECK YES OR NO FOR EACH ITEM)

Yes	No		
☐ 1	☐ 2	a.	Insufficient capital to install new source reduction equipment or implement new source reduction practices
☐ 1	☐ 2	b.	Lack of technical information on source reduction techniques applicable to the specific production processes
☐ 1	☐ 2	c.	Source reduction is not economically feasible: cost savings in waste management or production will not recover the capital investment
☐ 1	☐ 2	d.	Concern that product quality may decline as a result of source reduction
☐ 1	☐ 2	e.	Technical limitations of the production processes
☐ 1	☐ 2	f.	Permitting burdens
☐ 1	☐ 2	g.	Source reduction previously implemented - additional reduction does not appear to be technically feasible
☐ 1	☐ 2	h.	Source reduction previously implemented - additional reduction does not appear to be economically feasible
☐ 1	☐ 2	i.	Source reduction previously implemented - additional reduction does not appear to be feasible due to permitting requirements
☐ 1	☐ 2	j.	Other (SPECIFY COMMENTS IN BOX BELOW)

E. Did any of the factors listed below delay or limit the site's ability to initiate new or additional on-site or off-site recycling activities during 1994 or 1995? (CHECK YES OR NO FOR EACH ITEM)

Yes	No			Yes	No		
☐ 1	☐ 2	a.	Insufficient capital to install new recycling equipment or implement new recycling practice	☐ 1	☐ 2	g.	Technical limitations of production processes inhibit shipments off-site for recycling
☐ 1	☐ 2	b.	Lack of technical information on recycling techniques applicable to this site's specific production process	☐ 1	☐ 2	h.	Technical limitations of production processes inhibit on-site recycling
				☐ 1	☐ 2	i.	Permitting burdens inhibit recycling
☐ 1	☐ 2	c.	Recycling is not economically feasible: cost savings in waste management will not recover the capital investment	☐ 1	☐ 2	j.	Lack of permitted off-site recycling facilities
				☐ 1	☐ 2	k.	Unable to identify a market for recycled materials
☐ 1	☐ 2	d.	Concern that product quality may decline as a result of recycling	☐ 1	☐ 2	l.	Recycling previously implemented - additional recycling does not appear to be technically feasible
☐ 1	☐ 2	e.	Requirements to manifest wastes inhibit shipments of off-site for recycling	☐ 1	☐ 2	m.	Recycling previously implemented - additional recycling does not appear to be economically feasible
☐ 1	☐ 2	f.	Financial liability provisions inhibit shipments off-site for recycling	☐ 1	☐ 2	n.	Recycling previously implemented - additional recycling does not appear to be feasible due to permitting requirements
				☐ 1	☐ 2	o.	Other (SPECIFY COMMENTS IN BOX BELOW)

Comments:

Appendix C-2

NCP COMPLIANCE CHECKLIST

Compliance with the National Contingency Plan (N.C.P.) is mandatory for recovery of your response costs under the powerful CERCLA statute (42 U.S.C. §9600, *et.seq.*), for your <u>private party</u> environmental actions (e.g., investigation, cleanup, closure).

<u>Is the NCP Applicable to Our Site?</u>

1)   Are there <u>any</u> response costs incurred or contemplated (i.e., any investigation and/or remediation)? YES ___   NO___

2)   Does the contamination include <u>anything</u> besides <u>solely</u> petroleum or asbestos (e.g., solvents, metals, PCBs)? YES ___ NO ___

"YES" MEANS THE <u>NCP PROBABLY APPLIES</u>! In other words, if you don't comply with the NCP, there is a high likelihood that you will be precluded from recovering response costs in some later (or pending) CERCLA lawsuit.

<u>Is Our Response Action Complying With the NCP?</u>

While there are literally hundreds of potentially applicable provisions from the complex NCP, the following represent a sampling of some of the more important time-bombs:

1)   Have we prepared a <u>written baseline risk assessment</u> (NCP §300.430(d)(4))? YES ___ NO ___

2)   Have we prepared a <u>written feasibility study</u> which includes the mandatory "no action" alternative (NCP §300.430(e))? YES ___ NO ___

3)   Have we provided a <u>formal public comment period prior</u> to selecting or implementing <u>any</u> part of the remedial action (NCP §300.430(f)(3)(C))? YES ___ NO ___

Appendix D-1

4)   Have we conducted a <u>transcribed public hearing</u> which must be officially noticed to the public and all PRPs <u>prior</u> to selecting or implementing <u>any</u> part of the remedial action (NCP §300.430(f)(3)(D))? YES ___ NO ___

"NO" MEANS AN <u>INABILITY TO RECOVER</u>! In other words, failure to comply with any of these key provisions probably may make it impossible for you to recover your <u>private party</u> environmental response costs under the powerful CERCLA laws.

PRELIMINARY ENVIRONMENTAL AUDIT FORM

Preparer:_____Title/Position: _____

Prepared for: _____ Date:_____

1.   Property Name: _____

2.   Owner(s): _____

3.   Address: _____

_____

4.   Neighbors: (all sides) _____

_____

5.   Tenant(s): _____

_____

6.   Structure(s): _____

_____

7.   Type(s) of Operations:_____

_____

8.   Previous Site Uses:_____

_____

PRELIMINARY ENVIRONMENTAL AUDIT FORM

9.   Environmental Risk Features:

   a.   Aboveground Tanks (number, size, age, type, contents):

   _____

   b.   Underground Tanks (number, approx. size, age, contents):

   _____

   c.   Sumps/Clarifiers: _____

   d.   Wastewater Pits, Ponds, Lagoons, Drainage Channels:

   _____

   e.   Evidence of Above Features Existing Historically (fuel pumps,

   vent pipes, foundations, etc.): _____

   _____

10.   Possible Asbestos-Containing Materials (ceiling tiles, insulation, floor

   tile, transite siding, fireproofing, etc., installed prior to 1978):

   _____

   _____

11.   Possible PCB-Containing Equipment (Transformers, circuit breakers,

   capacitors, heat transfer systems, hydraulic systems and other electrical

   equipment which doesn't have "No PCB" labels): _____

   _____

   _____

PRELIMINARY ENVIRONMENTAL AUDIT FORM

12.   Chemicals Used or Stored: _____

_____

13.   Paints/Solvents Used or Stored: _____

_____

14.   Fifty-Five (55) Gallon Drums (include contents, if known):

_____

15.   Liquid Discharges From Buildings (to sewer, surface water or ditch):

_____

16.   Staining on Building(s):_____

_____

17.   Staining of Surface Soil:_____

_____

18.   Evidence of Spills or Leaks:_____

_____

19.   Disfigured, Discolored, Dying or Absence of Plant Life:_____

_____

Describe other features of the property and adjoining properties which might
pose an environmental concern, or provide additional information on any of the
above items: _____

_____

_____

Appendix E-3

MASTER CONSULTING AGREEMENT EXAMPLE

Prepared in anticipation of litigation or trial.
(Attorney-Client Privileged; Attorney Work-Product Protected).

This Master Consulting Agreement ("Agreement") is made and entered into
between _____ ("Law Firm"), _____ ("Client"), and
_____ ("Consultant"). This Agreement is primary and master to the
services agreement ("Underlying Agreement") entered into on or about this date
between Client and Consultant (attached hereto as Exhibit "A").   In
consideration of the mutual agreements herein contained, it is agreed as follows:

1.   EFFECTIVE DATE. The effective date of this Agreement is the date
        of execution for the Underlying Agreement.

2.   DESCRIPTION OF WORK. Consultant shall provide litigation
        consulting and related geo-environmental services regarding
        _____ (the "Work"). The precise scope of the
        geo-environmental services is reflected in the Underlying Agreement
        and any addendum thereto.

3.   INDEPENDENT CONTRACTOR RELATIONSHIP. In the
        performance of the Work, Consultant is and shall remain an
        independent contractor with the sole authority to control and direct the
        performance of the details of the Work, Law Firm being interested only
        in the results obtained. Consultant shall, at its expense, furnish such
        personnel, equipment, supplies and services as Consultant may deem
        necessary, in its sole discretion, for the performance and completion of
        the Work, Law Firm having no obligation in such matters whatsoever.
        The Work shall, however, be subject to Law Firm's review to monitor
        the satisfactory completion thereof.

4.   LAW FIRM'S AGENCY RELATIONSHIP. In entering into and
        executing the provisions of this Agreement, Law Firm is acting as
        agent for Client only. Law Firm has no independent liability to
        Consultant under this Agreement.

5.   PAYMENT.   Client shall pay all obligations to Consultant for
        services rendered pursuant to the Underlying Agreement. All parties
        agree that Law Firm is not in any fashion responsible for payments
        related to Consultant's services rendered.

Appendix F-1

6. INDEMNIFICATION. All parties agree that Law Firm is the agent of Client and is therefore equally entitled to all benefits of any indemnifications by Consultant to Client.

7. PRIVILEGED AND CONFIDENTIAL WORK PRODUCT. Consultant's performance of the Work under this Agreement is being conducted at the request of Law Firm in its capacity as legal counsel for Client in anticipation and/or in furtherance of litigation. All Work is intended to and shall constitute privileged and confidential attorney work-product. These provisions shall remain binding obligations on Consultant after the completion, expiration or termination of this Addendum. All documents, materials and other information developed, generated or prepared by or for Consultant in connection with the Work, except that forwarded directly to third parties such as governmental agencies, shall be marked "Prepared in Anticipation of Litigation or Trial. (Attorney-Client Privileged; Attorney Work-Product Protected)."

8. TERMINATION. Either party may, upon three (3) days written notice, terminate this Agreement, with or without cause. Such termination shall not impact the performance or enforcement of the Underlying Agreement.

9. CONFLICT. The provisions of this Agreement shall control over any conflict between the provisions hereof and any previous or subsequent oral or written agreement between the parties, absent a specific written alteration of this Agreement.

10. ENTIRE AGREEMENT. This is the entire agreement between the parties hereto and it can only be amended in a writing signed by all parties.

11. SEVERABILITY. In the event that a court determines any part of this Agreement is void or unenforceable, all other terms of this Agreement shall remain in full force and effect.

12. APPLICABLE LAW. This Agreement shall be construed in accordance with the laws of the State of _____, with venue proper only in _____.

13.   EXECUTION IN COUNTERPARTS. The parties may execute this
      Agreement in counterparts, each one of which will be an original or the
      equivalent thereof, but such counterparts together shall constitute but
      one and the same Agreement.

      IN WITNESS WHEREOF, the parties have executed this Agreement.

LAW FIRM   CONSULTANT   CLIENT
(_____)   (_____)   (_____)

_____   _____   _____

By: _____   By: _____   By: _____

Title: _____ Title: _____   Title: _____

Date: _____   Date: _____   Date: _____

PHASE I CONSULTANT SELECTION CHECKLIST

COMPANY			
All Historical Sources Reviewed (all 8 ASTM Listed Sources)			
All Historical Reviewed Back As Far As "Available"			
Fixed Set Price			
Chronological Historical Table (Summarizes All History of Site)			
Employees Complete <u>All</u> Work (<u>Not</u> Subcontractors)			
Concise, Next Step Actions with Associated Costs			
All <u>Local Regulatory</u> Agency Files Reviewed			
Complete 1 Mile Radius Regulatory Database Review (Not Transaction Screen)			
Photographs Documenting Entire Site (Sets Baseline With Minimum 6 Inside and 6 Outside Photographs)			
Site Interviews with Notes and Discussion			
Environmental Professional Liability Insurance: 2 Million Minimum with Best Company Rated "A" or Better			
Executive Summary - First Section of Report "Summarizes all Concerns & Facts			
Facts in Tables with Narrative Explanation for Easy Reading			
All Sources Revealed with Contact Names and Telephone Numbers Adding Credibility			

Appendix G

ASSESSING CURRENT FACILITY
OPERATIONS CHECKLIST

In preparing to assess current operations at a facility, certain procedures can be helpful in helping assure a successful assessment. The following is a checklist of appropriate measures in this regard:

____ Interviews with employees that are knowledgeable about the materials and processes used within each department.

____ Standardized questionnaire prepared to be used or distributed to employees to maintain consistency in the information that is gathered.

____ Facility surveyed and all materials present noted with their name and location.

____ Every department reviewed to determine how they handle hazardous wastes.

____ Appearance of facility and the areas where hazardous waste are generated and stored should be reviewed for the following:

   ____ Are hazardous wastes properly labeled in accumulation and storage areas?

   ____ Are employees taking proper precautions when handling hazardous wastes?

   ____ Do employees who handle hazardous waste have adequate training?

   ____ Are hazardous waste storage areas properly labeled and constructed?

____ Have employees been questioned on the handling, storage and disposal procedures for hazardous wastes, including:

   ____ Are any hazardous wastes being mishandled as non-hazardous waste?

   ____ Are hazardous wastes being generated where there is no documentation of its disposal?

Appendix H-1

ACCESSING CURRENT FACILITY
OPERATIONS CHECKLIST

____ Reviewed stored chemicals to determine if any have expired shelf lives.

____ Reviewed all records concerning hazardous materials and hazardous waste including:

    ____ Are material safety data sheets available for all chemicals used at the facility?

    ____ Are hazardous waste manifests available for at least the past three years?

    ____ Does the facility have the U.S. EPA Identification Number and is it used correctly on hazardous waste documentation?

    ____ Do transporters and disposal facilities that the facility uses for its hazardous waste have their own U.S. EPA Identification Numbers?

FACILITY INFORMATION WORKSHEET

	Complete? (Yes/No)	Current? (Yes/No)	Last Revision	Used in This Report? (Yes/No)	Document Identifi- cation	Location
A. Regulary Information						
Waste shipment manifests						
Emission inventories						
Hazardous waste reports						
Waste analyses						
Wastewater analyses						
Air emissions analyses						
Environment al audit reports						
Permits and/or permit applications						
Safety date sheets						
OSHA requirements and inspections						
B. Process Information						
Material safety data sheets						

Appendix I-1

FACILITY INFORMATION WORKSHEET

Product and raw material inventory records						
Operator data logs						
Operating codes/manual						
Operating schedules						
Work flow diagrams						
Plot and elevation plans						
Equipment lists						
Equipment specification sheets						
Piping, wiring, and instrument diagrams						
Production records						
Inventory records						
Equipment layout plans						
Assays and analyses sheets						
Work flow diagrams						

FACILITY INFORMATION WORKSHEET

	Complete? (Yes/No)	Current? '(Yes/No)	Last Revision	Used in This Report? (Yes/No)	Document Identification	Location
Design and actual material, water and heat balances for Operating processes						
Design and actual material, water and heat balances for Pollution control processes						
C. Company Information						
Environmental policy statements						
Standard procedures						
Organizational charts						
D. Accounting Information						
Waste handling, treatment, and disposal costs						
Water and sewer costs, including surcharges						

Appendix I-3

FACILITY INFORMATION WORKSHEET

Product, energy, and raw material costs						
Operating and maintenance costs						
Department cost account reports						

CHARACTERIZING INDIVIDUAL
WASTE STREAMS WORKSHEET

Description of waste stream
Process unit/operation
Waste characteristics (attach additional sheets with composition and physical characteristic data as necessary)
□ gas □ liquid □ solid □ mixed phase
Assay
Density, g/cc
Viscosity/consistency
pH Flash point Water (%)
Other:
Waste leaving process: □ gaseous emission □ waste water □ solid waste □ hazardous waste
Occurrence
□ continuous
□ intermittent (complete below)
Type: □ periodic length of period:
□ sporadic (irregular occurrence)
□ non-recurrent
Generation rate
Annual (units___/time period___)
Maximum (units___/time period___)
Average (units___/time period___)

Appendix J-1

CHARACTERIZING INDIVIDUAL
WASTE STREAMS WORKSHEET

Frequency	(units____/time period____)
Disposal Frequency	
Applicable Federal, State, and local regulations (e.g., RCRA, TSCA, etc.)	
Management Location ☐ onsite ☐ offsite	
Describe:	
Disposal ☐ landfill	
☐ wastewater pond	
☐ waste pile	
☐ tailings impoundment	
☐ other (describe)	

CHARACTERIZING INDIVIDUAL
WASTE STREAMS WORKSHEET

Treatment	□ biological
	□ oxidation/reduction
	□ incineration
	□ pH adjustment
	□ precipitation
	□ other (describe)
	□ residue disposal/repository
Recycling	□ direct use/re-use, e.g., tails dewatering
	□ energy recovery
	□ other (describe)

CHARACTERIZING INDIVIDUAL
WASTE STREAMS WORKSHEET

Costs as of _____ (quarter and year)		
Cost element:	Unit price $ per _____	Reference/ source:
Onsite storage and handling		
Pretreatment		
Container		
Transportation Fee		
Disposal Fee		
Reclamation		
Local Taxes		
State Taxes		
Federal Taxes		
Other		
Total disposal cost		
Waste Origins/Sources		
Is the waste mixed with other wastes? □ Yes □ No If yes, fill out a sheet for each of the individual waste streams.		
Describe how the waste is generated, e.g., spill or leak cleanup, evaporative losses from heap or dump leaches, waste rock, slags lost from casting, leach solution from leaking pumps, etc. Attach flowsheets for clarity where appropriate.		

DESCRIPTION OF INPUT MATERIALS WORKSHEET

	Description		
	Stream No.	Stream No.	Stream No.
Name of material			
Source/Supplier			
Component/attribute of concern			
Annual consumption rate			
Overall			
Component(s) of concern			
Purchase price, $ per____			
Overall annual cost			
Method of delivery mode[1]			
Shipping container size and type[2]			

---

[1] For example, by pipeline, tank car, tank truck, truck, etc.

[2] For example, 10 gallon container, bay, etc.

Appendix K-1

DESCRIPTION OF INPUT MATERIALS WORKSHEET

Method of storage[3]			
Method of transfer[4]			
Empty container disposal mgmt.[5]			
Shelf life			
Supplier will			
- accept expired material? (Yes/No)			
- accept shipping containers? (Yes/No)			
- revise expiration date? (Yes/No)			
Acceptable substitute(s), if any			
Alternate supplier(s)			

---

[3] For example, outdoor storage, warehouse storage, underground/aboveground tank, etc.

[4] For example, by pump, forklift, pneumatic transport, conveyor, etc.

[5] For example, by crush and landfill, clean and recycle, return to supplier, etc.

POTENTIAL OPTIONS FOR MINIMIZING
HAZARDOUS WASTE WORKSHEET

Identification of waste stream:			
Coordinator of meeting:			
Meeting participants:			
Name	Title	Department	Telephone

List suggestion options	Rationale/remarks for options

Enter each above option on a separate Option Description Worksheet

Appendix L

DESCRIPTION OF A SPECIFIC WASTE MINIMIZATION OPTION WORKSHEET

Suggestion option (from the Option Generation Worksheet)
Briefly describe the option:
Waste stream(s) affected:
Input material(s) affected:
Product(s) affected:
Indicate type:
☐ Equipment-Related
☐ Personnel/Procedure-Related
☐ Materials-Related
Originally proposed by: Date:
Reviewed by: Date:
Approved for study? ☐ Yes   ☐ No   By:
Reasoning for acceptance or rejection for further study:
Following screening of these options by management, proceed to Technical/Environmental and Economic Feasibility Worksheets.

Appendix M

EQUIPMENT-RELATED
FEASIBILITY WORKSHEET
(Page 1 of 6)

Availability		
Equipment available commercially?	☐ Yes	☐ No
Demonstrated at another operation?	☐ Yes	☐ No
In similar application?	☐ Yes	☐ No
Successfully?	☐ Yes	☐ No
Describe closest analogous use:		
Describe status of development:		
Prospective Vendor Sources	Other Facility With Similar Vendor Equipment	Contact Person(s) at Operation

Appendix N-1

Other Facility(ies) with Similar Equipment	Contact Person(s) at Operation

Performance information required (describe parameters):

Environmental considerations

Are indirect environmental tradeoffs going to be experienced?
☐ Yes ☐ No

If yes, explain:

Testing required	☐ Yes ☐ No

Nature of testing:

Scale: ☐ bench   ☐ pilot   ☐ other

Test unit available?   ☐ Yes ☐ No

Test parameters (list):

Testing location: ☐ At operation

☐ Other

EQUIPMENT-RELATED
FEASIBILITY WORKSHEET
(Page 3 of 6)

Facility/production constraints
Space requirements:
Possible locations within facility:
Adequate existing facilities?
☐ Yes
☐ No. Explain solution:
Utility requirements
Electric power: Volts (AC or DC);   kW:
Process water: Flow: Pressure:
Quality (tap, demineralized, etc.):
Fuel: Type: Flow:
Duty:
Other:

Supply requirements
Describe significant changes in supplies required, e.g. chemicals, replacement parts, etc.

Items	Rate or Frequency of Replacement

Procurement requirements

Estimated lead times (after award of contracts):

Estimated installation and assembly time:

Proposed installation date:

Appendix N-4

EQUIPMENT-RELATED
FEASIBILITY WORKSHEET
(Page 5 of 6)

Production considerations
Will production be affected? Explain the effect and impact on production.
Will product quality be affected? Explain the effect on quality.
Will operations modifications to the flowsheet production procedures be required? Explain.
Maintenance considerations
How is service handled (maintenance and technical assistance)?
What warranties are offered?

EQUIPMENT-RELATED
FEASIBILITY WORKSHEET
(Page 6 of 6)

Storage considerations

Describe additional storage or material handling requirements.

Other significant requirements

Describe additional laboratory or analytical requirements.

Does this option appear technically and environmentally feasible, based upon the above?

☐ Yes ☐ No

PERSONNEL/PROCEDURE WORKSHEET
(Page 1 of 2)

What are the affected departments and areas?
Does each affected department and area believe the proposed change is feasible? ☐ Yes ☐ No
If not, why?
What applications changes are required?
What effect will the option have on health and safety requirements?
Training requirements:
Number to train on-site: operations   maintenance   other
Number to train off-site: operations   maintenance   other
Nature and duration of training:
What staffing changes are required?
Is union approval required?   Will the union approve?
Are indirect environmental tradeoffs going to experienced?
☐ Yes ☐ No   If yes, explain:
What operating instruction changes are necessary? Describe the effects on the responsible departments:

Appendix N-7

PERSONNEL/PROCEDURE WORKSHEET
(Page 2 of 2)

How will the regulatory permits be affected?
Does this option appear technically and environmentally feasible, based upon the above?   ☐ Yes ☐ No

Prepared by:_____   Date:_____

MATERIALS-RELATED
FEASIBILITY WORKSHEET
(Page 1 of 3)

Has the new material been demonstrated commercially? ☐ Yes ☐ No
In a similar application? ☐ Yes ☐ No
Successfully? ☐ Yes ☐ No
Describe closest analogous use:
What are the affected departments and areas? Do they believe the proposed change is feasible?
Will production quantity be affected? Explain the effect and the impact on production.
Will production quality be affected? Explain the effect on quality.

Will additional storage, handling, or other ancillary equipment be required? Explain.

Describe any training or procedure changes that are required.

Describe any material testing program that will be required.

What are the worker safety and health considerations, if any?

What indirect environmental tradeoffs are going to be experienced?

What effects will the new materials have on the number and toxicity of existing waste streams?

MATERIALS-RELATED
FEASIBILITY WORKSHEET
(Page 3 of 3)

What are the risks of material transfer to other media?
What are the environmental impacts of the input materials being proposed?
Does this option appear technically and environmentally feasible, based upon the above? ☐ Yes ☐ No

COST ESTIMATION WORKSHEET

Operating Cost/Revenue Item	$ per Year
Operating Costs	
Decrease (or increase) in disposal	
Decrease (or increase) in raw materials	
Decrease (or increase) in utility	
Decrease (or increase) in quality	
Decrease (or increase) in labor	
Decrease (or increase) in supplies	
Decrease (or increase) in insurance	
Decrease (or increase) in overhead	
Total decrease (or increase) in operating cost	
Revenue	
Incremental revenue from increased (decreased) production	
Incremental revenue from marketable by-products	
Net incremental revenue change:	
Units of production (annual)	
Annual net operating cost savings (loss)	
Enter annual net operating cost savings on Profitability Worksheet.	

CAPITAL COSTS WORKSHEET
(Page 1 of 2)

Capital Cost Item	Cost
Direct costs	
Site development	
Process equipment	
Materials	
Utilities and services	
Other non-process	
Construction/installation	
Indirect costs	
Engineering, design, procurement	
Permitting	
Contractor's fee	
Start-up costs	
Training costs	
Contingency	
Interest accrued during construction	
Total Fixed Capital Costs	
Working capital	
Raw material inventory	
Finished product inventory	
Materials and supplies	

CAPITAL COSTS WORKSHEET (2 of 2)

Total Working Capital	
Total Capital Investment	
Salvage value adjustment	
Total Capital Investment (adjusted)	
Enter total capital investment on Profitability Worksheet	

PROFITABILITY WORKSHEET

Total capital investment ($ from Capital Cost Worksheet)
Annual net operating cost savings ($ per year from Operating Cost Worksheet)
Total operating cost ($/unit)

$$\text{Payback period} \quad = \quad \frac{\text{Total capital investment}}{\text{Annual net operating cost savings}}$$

$$=$$

$$= \underline{\qquad} \text{ years}$$

Discounted cash flow rate of return can be investigated at this point. Several texts are available applying this technique, e.g., "Economic Evaluation and Investment Decision Methods," 8th Edition, by F.J. Stermole and J.M. Stermole, May 1993, Investment Evaluations Corporation, Golden, Colorado.

Appendix O-4

C.F.R. HAZARDOUS MATERIALS TABLE
(With Examples Relevant to the Precious Metals Industry)
Excerpts from 49 C.F.R. § 172.101

Symbols (1)	Hazardous materials descriptions and proper shipping names (2)	Hazard class or Division (3)	Identification Numbers (4)	Packing group (5)	Label(s) required (if not excepted) (6)	Special Provisions (7)	Packaging authorizations (§ 173.***)			Quantity limitations		Vessel stowage requirements (10)	
							Exceptions (8A)	Non-bulk packaging (8B)	Bulk packaging (8C)	Passenger aircraft or railcar (9A)	Cargo aircraft only (9B)	Vessel stowage (10A)	Other stowage provisions (10B)
....	Cyanide solutions	6.1	UN1935	I II III	POISON POISON KEEP AWAY FROM FOOD	B37, T18, T26 / T18, T26 / T18, T26	None None 153	201 202 203	243 243 241	1 L 5 L 60 L	30 L 60 L 220 L	B A A	40, 52 40, 52 40, 52
....	Hydrochloric acid, solution	8	UN1789	II	CORROSIVE	A3, A6, B3 B15, N41, T9 T27	154	202	242	1 L	30 L	C	8
....	Nitrating acid mixtures *with 50 per cent or more nitric acid.*	8	UN1796	I	CORROSIVE, OXIDIZER	T12, T27	None	158	243	Forbidden	2.5 L	D	40, 66 89

Appendix P-1

C.F.R. HAZARDOUS WARNING LABELS (Examples)

Excerpts from 49 C.F.R. § 172.552 - 172.560

Symbols	Hazardous materials descriptions and proper shipping names	Hazard class or Division	Identification Numbers	Packing group	Label(s) required (if not excepted)	Special Provisions	Packaging authorizations (§ 173. ***)			Quantity limitations		Vessel stowage requirements	
							Exceptions	Non-bulk packaging	Bulk packaging	Passenger aircraft or railcar	Cargo aircraft only	Vessel stowage	Other stowage provisions
(1)	(2)	(3)	(4)	(5)	(6)	(7)	(8A)	(8B)	(8C)	(9A)	(9B)	(10A)	(10B)
....	Oxidizing substances, liquid, n.o.s.	5.1	UN3139	II	OXIDIZER	A2	152	202	242	1 L	5 L	B	56, 58, 69, 106
....	Potassium cyanide	6.1	UN1680	I	POISON	B69, B77, N74, N75, T18, T26	None	211	242	5 kg	50 kg	B	52
....	Sodium cyanide	6.1	UN1689	I	POISON	B69, B77, N74, N75, T42	None	211	242	5 kg	50 kg	B	52

Appendix P-2

C.F.R. HAZARDOUS WARNING LABELS (Examples)
Excerpts from 49 C.F.R. §172.552 - 172.560

Appendix Q

SAMPLE SCENARIOS REGARDING
TRANSPORTATION OF HAZARDOUS
MATERIALS TO RECLAIM PRECIOUS METALS

The following is a list of scenarios where hazardous materials are generated and the related requirements are proposed for shipment off-site in order to reclaim significant amounts of precious metals that they contain:

Sample Case 1

A cyanide solution (400 gallons) designed to strip gold can no longer be utilized because it is spent. Sodium cyanide is an active ingredient and the bath has a pH of 12.5 or higher.

Proper Shipping Name:	RQ Waste Corrosive Liquid, Poisonous, 8, UN2922, PG 1, Corrosive, Poison (RQ Sodium Cyanide - F009)
EPA Waste Numbers:	F009, D002
Labels:	Poison, Corrosive, Hazardous Waste
Packaging:	Specification 6D Drums. (Polyethylene lined steel)
Shipping Paper:	Hazardous Waste Manifest with Landfill Ban Form Attached
Emergency Response Guide Reference:	#55 (Attach to manifest with LB form)

Sample Case 2

A potassium cyanide plating bath (200 gallons) utilized to plate gold can no longer be utilized and contains significant amounts of precious metals in solution. The pH of the solution is 6.0.

Proper Shipping Name:	RQ Waste Potassium Cyanide Solution, 5.1. UN1680, PG I, Poison (RQ Potassium Cyanide - F007)
EPA Waste Numbers:	F007
Labels:	Poison, Hazardous Waste
Packaging:	Specification 6D Drums.
Shipping Paper:	Hazardous Waste Manifest with Landfill Ban Form Attached
Emergency Response Guide Reference:	#55

Sample Case 3

Two opened (seal broken) Polyethylene one gallon jars (40 pounds) of virgin potassium gold cyanide salts are unusable because they are of specification where they have existed past the recommended expiration date.

Proper Shipping Name:	RQ Waste Potassium Cyanide, 6.1, UN1680, PG I, Poison (RQ Potassium Cyanide - P098)
EPA Waste Numbers:	P098
Labels:	Poison, Hazardous Waste
Packaging:	Polyethylene Salvage Container (DOT Approved E9618 or E10242)
Shipping Paper:	Hazardous Waste Manifest, LB Form attached
Emergency Response Guide Reference:	#55

Sample Case 4

The filters, pump parts, and other equipment components resulting from the maintenance of a potassium and sodium cyanide plating bath have significant amounts of gold plated onto their surfaces or imbedded as particulate in the respective subsurface. A mixture of cyanides are present (less than one pound total).

Proper Shipping Name:	Waste Cyanides, inorganic, n.o.s., UN1588, 6.1, PGIII (Reactive cyanides - D003, F007)
EPA Waste Numbers:	D003, F007
Labels:	Hazardous Waste, Keep Away From Food
Packaging:	Specification 17H or 17C Drum
Shipping Paper:	Hazardous Waste Manifest
Emergency Response Guide Reference:	#55

Sample Case 5

In a laboratory, nitric acid is utilized to dissolve base metals in order to perform an analysis for silver metal. There are four drums of 20 percent nitric acid (200 gallons) which contain 39 pounds total of silver nitrate. Some of the samples which were dissolved are alloys that contained selenium and cadmium in small amounts. (Note: Refer to the State environmental regulations to determine if the material is managed as a hazardous waste.)

Proper Shipping Name:	RQ (Waste) Oxidizing Substances, Liquid, Corrosive, NOS, 5.1, UN3098, PGII, Oxidizer (RQ Silver Nitrate - D011, D003; Cadmium - D006, Selenium - D010)
EPA Waste Numbers:	D003, D011, D006, D010 (If lead is present add D008, mercury D009, etc.)
Labels:	Hazardous Waste and/or Oxidizer
Packaging:	Stainless Steel Specification 17E Drums
Shipping Paper:	Hazardous Waste Manifest or Approved Shipping Paper (With attached landfill ban form)
Emergency Response Guide Reference:	#60

Sample Case 6

In a metal treatment facility a 60% nitric acid mixture (50 gallons) is utilized with an additive to dissolve strip gold alloys from refractory metal surfaces. (Note: Refer to State environmental regulations to determine if this material is managed as a hazardous waste.)

Proper Shipping Name:	(Waste) Nitrating acid Mixture (with 50% or more nitric acid), 8, UN1796, PG I, Corrosive, Oxidizer
EPA Waste Numbers:	D001, D002, D003
Labels:	Hazardous Waste and/or Oxidizer
Packaging:	Stainless Steel Specification 17E Drums
Shipping Paper:	Hazardous Waste Manifest or Approved Shipping Paper with Landfill Ban Form Attached
Emergency Response Guide Reference:	#44

Sample Case 7

In a metal fabrication plant precious metal surfaces are polished and cut, generating fine particulate that contains small amounts of soluble lead and cadmium metals. (note: Refer to State environmental regulations to determine if the material is managed as a waste.)

Proper Shipping Name:	Hazardous Waste, Solid, Environmentally Hazardous Substances, 9, NA3077, PGIII
EPA Waste Numbers:	D006, D008
Labels:	Hazardous Waste and/or Class 9
Packaging:	Specification 17H or 17C
Shipping Paper:	Hazardous Waste Manifest and/or Approved Shipping Paper with the Landfill Ban Form Attached

Sample Case 8

In a gold refinery, aqua regia is used to dissolve metal alloys. After removing the nitrates and precipitating the gold, there are platinum group metals in solution (50 gallons) which are shipped off-site to a PGM refinery. (Note: Refer to State environmental regulations to determine if the material managed as a hazardous waste.)

Proper Shipping Name:	Waste Hydrochloric acid, Solution, 9, UN1789, PGII Corrosive
EPA Waste Numbers:	D002
Labels:	Hazardous Waste and/or Corrosive
Packaging:	Specification 34 Polyethylene Drum
Shipping Paper:	Hazardous Waste Manifest and/or Approved Shipping Paper with Landfill Ban Form Attached
Emergency Response Guide Reference:	#60

Source: Charles S. Tatakis (Handy & Harmon), "How to Get it from Here to There Correctly and Safely," IPMI Environmental Workshop (January 1994, Arlington, Virginia).

NOTIFICATION OF REGULATED WASTE ACTIVITY FORM
(1 of 2)

Please print or type with ELITE type (12 characters per inch) in the unshaded areas only

Form Approved, OMB No. 2050-0028 Expires 9-30-96
GSA No. 0246-EPA-OT

Please refer to the *Instructions for Filling Notification before completing this form.* The information requested here is required by law (Section 3010 of the *Resource Conservation and Recovery Act*).

⊕EPA Notification of Regulated Waste Activity

United States Environmental Protection Agency

Date Received
(For Official Use Only)

I. Installation's EPA ID Number (Mark 'X' in the appropriate box)

☐ A. First Notification   ☐ B. Subsequent Notification (Complete Item C)

C. Installation's EPA ID Number

II. Name of Installation (Include company and specific site name)

III. Location of Installation (Physical address not P.O. Box or Route Number)

Street

Street (Continued)

City or Town   State   Zip Code   —

County Code   County Name

IV. Installation Mailing Address (See Instructions)

Street or P.O. Box

City or Town   State   Zip Code   —

V. Installation Contact (Person to be contacted regarding waste activities at site)

Name (Last)   (First)

Job Title   Phone Number (Area Code and Number)   —   —

VI. Installation Contact Address (See Instructions)

A. Contact Address
Location   Mailing   Other   B. Street or P.O. Box

City or Town   State   Zip Code   —

VII. Ownership (See Instructions)

A. Name of Installation's Legal Owner

Street, P.O. Box, or Route Number

City or Town   State   Zip Code   —

Phone Number (Area Code and Number)   —   — | B. Land Type | C. Owner Type | D. Change of Owner Indicator Yes / No | (Date Changed) Month Day Year |

EPA Form 8700-12 (Rev. 11-30-93) Previous edition is obsolete.

Continued on Reverse

Appendix S-1

NOTIFICATION OF REGULATED WASTE ACTIVITY FORM
(2 of 2)

Please print or type with ELITE type (12 characters per inch) in the unshaded areas only

Form Approved, OMB No. 2050-0028 Expires 9-30-96
GSA No. 0246-EPA-OT

ID - For Official Use Only

VIII. Type of Regulated Waste Activity (Mark 'X' in the appropriate boxes; Refer to Instructions)

A. Hazardous Waste Activity

1. **Generator (See Instructions)**
   - a. Greater than 1000kg/mo (2,200 lbs.)
   - b. 100 to 1000 kg/mo (200-2,200 lbs.)
   - c. Less than 100 kg/mo (220 lbs)
2. **Transporter (Indicate Mode in boxes 1-5 below)**
   - a. For own waste only
   - b. For commercial purposes

   Mode of Transportation
   - 1. Air
   - 2. Rail
   - 3. Highway
   - 4. Water
   - 5. Other - specify

3. **Treater, Storer, Disposer (at Installation)** Note: A permit is required for this activity; see instructions.
4. **Hazardous Waste Fuel**
   - a. Generator Marketing to Burner
   - b. Other Marketers
   - c. Boiler and/or Industrial Furnace
     - 1. Smelter Deferral
     - 2. Small Quantity Exemption Indicate Type of Combustion Device(s)
       - 1. Utility Boiler
       - 2. Industrial Boiler
       - 3. Industrial Furnace
5. **Underground Injection Control**

B. Used Oil Recycling Activities

1. **Used Oil Fuel Marketer**
   - a. Marketer Directs Shipment of Used Oil to Off-Specification Burner
   - b. Marketer Who First Claims the Used Oil Meets the Specifications
2. **Used Oil Burner - Indicate Type(s) of Combustion Device(s)**
   - a. Utility Boiler
   - b. Industrial Boiler
   - c. Industrial Furnace
3. **Used Oil Transporter - Indicate Type(s) of Activity(ies)**
   - a. Transporter
   - b. Transfer Facility
4. **Used Oil Processor/Re-refiner - Indicate Type(s) of Activity(ies)**
   - a. Process
   - b. Re-refine

IX. Description of Hazardous Wastes (Use additional sheets if necessary)

A. Characteristics of Nonlisted Hazardous Wastes. (Mark 'X' in the boxes corresponding to the characteristics of nonlisted hazardous wastes your installation handles; See 40 CFR Parts 261.20 - 261.24)

1. Ignitable (D001)	2. Corrosive (D002)	3. Reactive (D003)	4. Toxicity Characteristic (List specific EPA hazardous waste number(s) for the Toxicity characteristic contaminant(s))

B. Listed Hazardous Wastes. (See 40 CFR 261.31 - 33; See instructions if you need to list more than 12 waste codes.)

1	2	3	4	5	6
7	8	9	10	11	12

C. Other Wastes. (State or other wastes requiring a handler to have an I.D. number; See instructions.)

1	2	3	4	5	6

X. Certification

I certify under penalty of law that this document and all attachments were prepared under my direction or supervision in accordance with a system designed to assure that qualified personnel properly gather and evaluate the information submitted. Based on my inquiry of the person or persons who manage the system, or those persons directly responsible for gathering the information, the information submitted is, to the best of my knowledge and belief, true, accurate, and complete. I am aware that there are significant penalties for submitting false information, including the possibility of fine and imprisonment for knowing violations.

Signature	Name and Official Title (Type or print)	Date Signed

XI. Comments

Note: Mail completed form to the appropriate EPA Regional or State Office. (See Section III of the booklet for addresses.)

EPA Form 8700-12 (Rev. 11-30-93) Previous edition is obsolete.

Appendix S-2

UNIFORM HAZARDOUS WASTE MANIFEST FORM

State of California—Environmental Protection Agency
Form Approved OMB No. 2050-0039 (Expires 9-30-96)
Please print or type.   Form designed for use on elite (12-pitch) typewriter.

Department of Toxic Substances Control
Sacramento, California

95940655

WITHIN CALIFORNIA, CALL 1-800-852-7550
GENERATOR 1-800-424-8802; WITHIN CALIFORNIA, CALL THE NATIONAL RESPONSE CENTER IN CASE OF EMERGENCY OR SPILL, CALL

UNIFORM HAZARDOUS WASTE MANIFEST	1. Generator's US EPA ID No.	Manifest Document No.	2. Page 1 of	Information in the shaded areas is not required by Federal law.

3. Generator's Name and Mailing Address

A. State Manifest Document Number **95940655**

B. State Generator's ID

4. Generator's Phone (   )

5. Transporter 1 Company Name   6. US EPA ID Number

C. State Transporter's ID

D. Transporter's Phone

7. Transporter 2 Company Name   8. US EPA ID Number

E. State Transporter's ID

F. Transporter's Phone

9. Designated Facility Name and Site Address   10. US EPA ID Number

G. State Facility's ID

H. Facility's Phone

11. US DOT Description (including Proper Shipping Name, Hazard Class, and ID Number)	12. Containers No.	Type	13. Total Quantity	14. Unit Wt/Vol	I. Waste Number
a.					State
					EPA / Other
b.					State
					EPA / Other
c.					State
					EPA / Other
d.					State
					EPA / Other

J. Additional Descriptions for Materials Listed Above

K. Handling Codes for Wastes Listed Above
a.   b.
c.   d.

15. Special Handling Instructions and Additional Information

16. GENERATOR'S CERTIFICATION: I hereby declare that the contents of this consignment are fully and accurately described above by proper shipping name and are classified, packed, marked, and labeled, and are in all respects in proper condition for transport by highway according to applicable international and national government regulations.

If I am a large quantity generator, I certify that I have a program in place to reduce the volume and toxicity of waste generated to the degree I have determined to be economically practicable and that I have selected the practicable method of treatment, storage, or disposal currently available to me which minimizes the present and future threat to human health and the environment; OR, if I am a small quantity generator, I have made a good faith effort to minimize my waste generation and select the best waste management method that is available to me and that I can afford.

Printed/Typed Name	Signature	Month	Day	Year

17. Transporter 1 Acknowledgement of Receipt of Materials

Printed/Typed Name	Signature	Month	Day	Year

18. Transporter 2 Acknowledgement of Receipt of Materials

Printed/Typed Name	Signature	Month	Day	Year

19. Discrepancy Indication Space

20. Facility Owner or Operator Certification of receipt of hazardous materials covered by this manifest except as noted in Item 19.

Printed/Typed Name	Signature	Month	Day	Year

DO NOT WRITE BELOW THIS LINE.

DTSC 8022A (1/95)
EPA 8700—22

White: TSDF SENDS THIS COPY TO DTSC WITHIN 30 DAYS.
To: P.O. Box 3000, Sacramento, CA 95812

Appendix T-1

DISASTER RECOVERY CONSULTANTS LIST

The following companies provide disaster recovery services in the United States:

Accolade Systems Konsultants, Inc.
Richard L. Whaley
801 W. State Road 436, Ste. 1079
Altamonte Springs, FL 32714
(407)682-2700, Fax (407)682-6089

Available and Secured Knowledge,
Consulting
Gerald Walter Grindler
PO Box 20170
St. Louis, MO 63123-0370
(800)621-3805, Fax (314)894-9784

Brown, Pistone, Hurley &
  Van Vlear
Michael Paul Hutchins, Esq., P.E.
8001 Irvine Center Drive, Suite 900
Irvine, CA 92718
(714)450-8433, Fax (714)727-0656

Chubb Services Corporation
Andrew Marks
25 Independence Boulevard
Warren, NJ 07059
(908)580-7181, Fax (908)580-7187

Comdisco Consulting Services
Edward J. Evans
6111 N. River Road
Rosemont, IL 60018
(708)698-3000, Fax (708)518-5242

Computer Security Consultants, Inc.
R.A. "Randy" March
590 Danbury Road
Ridgefield, CT 06877
(203)431-8720, Fax (203)431-8165

Contingency Management Consulting
Johne E. Laye
346 Rheem Blvd, Ste. 202
Moraga, CA 94556
(510)631-0400, Fax (510)631-0403

Data Guard Recovery Services, Inc.
Dianna L. Jansen
PO Box 37144
Louisville, KY 40233-7144
(800)325-3977, Fax (502)426-3028

Data Processing Security, Inc.
Louis Scoma, Jr.
200 East Loop 820
Fort Worth, TX 76112
(817)457-9400 ext. 216, Fax
(817)457-9400

David E. Scarbrough, Inc.
David E. Scarbrough
1720 Belgrade Drive
Plano, TX 75023
(214)867-1604

Exchange Resources, Inc.
Ken Israel
5700 Green Circle Drive
Minneapolis, MN 55343

Hewlett-Packard
Cheryl Johannes
19091 Pruneridge Avenue, 46 UP
Cupertino, CA 95014
(408)447-7588, Fax (408)447-4208

IBM Business Recovery Consultation
Services
Marcia A. Carpenter
Long Meadow Road
PO Box 700
Sterling Forest, NY 10970-0700
(914)759-4433, Fax (914)759-4690

Information Integrity
Charles Cresson Wood
PO Box 1219
Sausalito, CA 94966
(415)332-7763, Fax (415)332-8032

Munters Moisture Control Services
Richard Freund
16 Hunt Road
Amesbury, MA 01913
(800)959-7901, Fax (508)388-4939

Page Assured Systems Inc.
Arthur E. Hutt
251-28 52nd Ave.
Little Neck, NY 11362
(718)428-0760, Fax (516)829-3977

PASE Inc.
Alan B. Bernstein
PO Box 1299
Highland Park, NJ 08904
(908)321-1011, Fax (908)321-1014

Persson Associates
Jan Persson
1524 Crabtree Lane, Ste. 100
Deerfield, IL 60015
(708)940-1660

Warrington & Associates, Inc.
Mark M. Warrington
1075 N.W. Murray Road, Suite 275
Portland, OR 07729
(503)292-0054, Fax (503)292-0054

Weyerhaeuser Recovery Services
Michael Pearce
33330 8th Avenue, South
Federal Way, WA 98003
(800)654-9347, Fax (206)727-7060

Data Assurance Corporation
Kimberly Shafer
12503 E. Euclid Drive, Suite 250
Englewood, CO 80111
(800)654-1689, Fax (303)792-0218

Miora Systems Consulting, Inc.
Michael Miora
PO Box 6028
Playa del Rey, CA 90296
(310)306-1365, Fax (310)305-1493

The following companies provide disaster recovery services both in the United States and foreign countries:

Aeroscopic Engineers, Inc.
Ian Spiszman
5245 San Fernando Road-West
Los Angeles, CA 90039
(800)950-2376
Fax (213)245-3028

AGS Federal Systems, Inc.
Michael Rodgers
11820 Parklawn Drive
Rockville, MD 20852
(301)770-4600
Fax (301)468-9221

Arel Technologies, Inc.
Joseph H. Arel
7111 W. Broadway
Minneapolis, MN 55428
(612)560-0203
Fax (612)560-2506

Caroline Pratt and Associates, Inc.
Caroline Pratt/Tom Wheeler
24104 Village 24
Camarillo, CA 93012
(800)678-7728
Fax (805)386-7005

Contingency Planning, Inc.
Glenn Dickey
PO Box 340157
Columbus, OH 43234
(614)761-8850
Fax (614)793-0092

CSC CompuSource
Marketing Services
118 Mackenan Drive, Suite 300
Cary, NC 27511
(800)671-2948

Data Clean Corporation
Peter Stamos
1070 Tower Lane
Bensenville, IL 60106
(708)860-7777
Fax (708)860-9471

Data Retrieval Services, Inc.
Carleen Bridgemen
1250 Rogers St., Suite C
Clearwater, FL 34616
(813)461-5900
Fax (813)461-5668

D.M. McNaughton Consulting Inc.
Don McNaughton
2281 Armcrescent West
Halifax, Nova Scotia, Canada
(902)422-3114

Disaster Survival Planning, Inc.
Judy Bell
669 Pacific Cove Dr.
Port Hueneme, CA 93041
(805)984-9547
(Worldwide)

Executive Compumetrics, Inc.
Stephen A. Gierach
PO Box 95
Tinley Park, IL 60477
(800)368-3324, (708)687-1150,
Fax (708)687-1183

The Kingswell Partnership, Inc.
Paul F. Kirvan
20 Gael Court, Ste. 100
(609)228-7525
Fax (609)232-8821
(U.S., Europe, Canada, Pacific
Rim)

Phoenix Consulting Services, Inc.
Edmond D. Jones
PO Box 777
Warren, MI 48090-0777
(313)739-4669
Fax (313)739-3901

Recovery Management, Inc.
Randall M. Coleman
435 King Street
Littleton, MA 01460
(508)486-8866, (508)486-0060

Recovery-Plus Planning Products
and Services
Jim Mannion
1806 E. Northwest Highway
Arlington Heights, Il 60004
(708)255-7400

Rothstein Associates, Inc.
Philip Jan Rothstein
13 Spring Pond Drive
Ossining, NY 10562-2000
(914)941-6867
Fax (914)923-4118

Sternudd Consulting AB
Jan G. Sternudd
PO Box 43
S-570 91 Kristdala, Sweden
Int +46-491-40088
Fax Int +46-491-40078

Strategic Technologies
International, Inc.
Gene Austin
5005 West Laurel Street
Suite 212
Tampa, FL 33607
(813)286-2007
Fax (813)282-4918

Strohl Systems
500 North Gulph Road, Suite 500
King of Prussia, PA 19406
(800)634-2016, (610)768-4120,
Fax (610)768-4135

SunGard Planning Solutions, Inc.
T.L. Sawicki
1285 Drummers Lane
Wayne, PA 19087
(800)448-6850
Fax (215)687-0108
(U.S., Canada)

TAMP Computer Systems Inc.
Thomas Abruzzo
1732 Remson Avenue
Merrick, NY 11566
(516)623-2038
Fax (516)223-2128

Technology and Management
Planning Associates
Steven B. Goldman
PO Box 617
Olney, MD 20830
(301)570-3588
Fax (301)570-5281

XL/Datacomp, Inc.
Sandy Lorenca
908 N. Elm Street
Hinsdale, IL 60521
(800)323-3289 ext. 2443
Fax (708)323-3871

Telehouse International
Corporation of America
Joe Ettore
6 Teleport Drive, The Teleport
Staten Island, NY 10311
(718)983-2500
Fax (718)983-2517
(U.S., Europe, Pacific Rim)

PLANNING SCENARIO,
NEWPORT-INGLEWOOD FAULT SUMMARY

The Earthquake Threat

The Newport-Inglewood Fault Zone (NIFZ) was the source of the destructive 1933 Long Beach earthquake of magnitude (M) 6.3. Other damaging earthquakes have occurred on the NIFZ, both before and after 1933.

The northwestern end of the NIFZ is near Beverly Hills. The NIFZ extends southeasterly to include the epicenter of the 1933 earthquake offshore from Newport Beach, and beyond. A major earthquake (M of about 7.0) on the NIFZ would strongly affect the Los Angeles metropolitan area. [The Los Angeles metropolitan area is defines as "...approximately 30 miles wide and bounded by the Pacific coast from Santa Monica to San Juan Capistrano on the west, and includes the cities of San Fernando, Pasadena, and Orange on the east. The area encompasses the vast majority of the 10 million people in Los Angeles and Orange counties.] The impact of such an event on the network of lifelines is addressed in this scenario.

The Scenario Earthquake

The scenario earthquake of M about 7 assumes subsurface faulting on the NIFZ from near Beverly Hills to offshore Laguna Beach, about 45 miles. Surface displacements averaging 1 to 3 feet (maximum 6 feet) occur on the discontinuous segments of active faults in the NIFZ. Potentially damaging shaking continues for about 25 seconds within 25 miles of the NIFZ. After shocks occur for weeks, with a few magnitude comparable to the Whittier Narrows earthquake (m 5.9) of October 1, 1987.

Because large earthquakes occur less frequently than small ones, the likelihood of occurrence of the scenario earthquake is in general lower than that of a M 6.3 event such as occurred in 1933. The scenario event provides a possible worst case for emergency planning.

Seismic Intensity Distribution

Intensity VIII or greater Modified Mercalli (damage to ordinary building and partial collapse of weak structures) extends throughout the alluvial sections of the Los Angeles basin to Monrovia and San Fernando, and coastal Orange County to San Juan Capistrano.

Intensity IX (considerable damage and partial collapse of ordinary buildings) occurs in the alluvial areas within 5 miles of the NIFZ.

Ground breakage could produce intensities greater that IX, in the 5 mile wide NIFZ, in the areas of potential liquefaction such as the harbors, and in areas of potential landslides such as the Santa Monica Mountains and Palos Verdes Hills.

Comparison to M8 Earthquake on the San Andreas Fault

The NIFZ is located within the Los Angeles metropolitan area, whereas the San Andreas fault (SAF) is more than 30 miles distant. Consequently, in the Los Angeles metropolitan area, the impact of an earthquake of M7 on the NIFZ is stronger than the impact of a M8 earthquake on the SAF.

Hospitals

Of the 155 acute care hospitals in Los Angeles and Orange counties, 143 are located in the planning area within 25 miles of the NIFZ, including 55 hospitals located within 5 miles of the NIFZ. It is estimated that 7,439 of the 13,000 beds within 5 miles of the NIFZ, will be unavailable due to damage, restricted access, and loss of utilities. In the zone from 5 to 25 miles from the NIFZ, bed loss is estimated at 25%. No bed loss occurs in the 12 hospitals (2,000 beds) at distances greater than 25 miles from the NIFZ. The total bed loss in Los Angeles and Orange counties is 14,439 of 43,000 beds available, or 34%.

Highways

Route 1 is damaged by a landslide at Pacific Palisades near Santa Monica, and by liquefaction at Marina Del Rey. Route 1 is open to emergency traffic in Long Beach, but closed south of there.

Route 22 (Garden Grove Freeway) is damaged at the interchange with Route 405 (San Diego Freeway).

Route 39 (Beach Boulevard) is damaged at the interchanges with Routes 405 and 22.

Liquefaction on the Terminal Island has damaged the approaches of 3 bridges: Vincent Thomas, Gerald Desmond, and the Schuyler Heim.

Route 101 (Hollywood Freeway) is blocked at the Hollywood Boulevard and Sunset Boulevard over-crossings.

Rupture of the roadway and utility pipelines near the Route 110 (Harbor Freeway)/El Segundo Boulevard interchange necessitates a lengthy detour.

Route 405 is blocked by a landslide in Sepulveda Canyon. Route 405 is closed from Route 110 to Route 605 (San Gabriel River Freeway), and from Route 22-East to Irvine.

Route 605 is partially closed south of the interchange with Route 91 (Artesia Freeway).

Route 701 (Long Beach Freeway) is closed between Route 91 and Long Beach.

Airports

Los Alamitos Armed Forces Reserve Center sustains significant damage to runways, fuel tanks, and other structures.

Long Beach International sustains significant damage to the control tower and other facilities, but the runways remain functional. Freeway damage (I-405) will impair access from the south.

Orange County (John Wayne) sustains damage to the control tower, runway, fuel tanks, and other structures. The runway damage may be repairable in 24 hours. Access will be limited by damage to State 55 and 73 and I-405.

Los Angeles International (LAX) sustains some damage to structures and facilities, but the runways remain functional. Damage to access routes, including the Century Boulevard/Sepulveda Boulevard interchange, will reduce the capacity of LAX to 30% for two days.

Railroads

Ground and rail failures occur in the Wilmington, Long Beach, and Seal Beach areas. The rail bridge to Terminal Island is closed.

The Los Angeles to Santa Monica line is closed by faulting at the bridge over Ballona Creek.

The lines from Los Angeles and from Watts to El Segundo are closed due to faulting and shaking damage to bridges.

Faulting closes the line from Compton to East Long Beach. The bridge at Route 710 crossing just west of the Los Angeles River is damaged.

The line into Seal Beach Navel Weapons Station is closed by faulting and liquefaction.

The Orange to San Diego line is closed due to liquefaction.

Los Angeles - Long Beach Harbor

Access to Terminal Island is limited to Ocean Boulevard across Gerald Desmond Bridge, because of approach failures at Vincent Thomas, and Schuyler Heim bridges.

In Long Beach, Route 710 is closed due to liquefaction, and access to the southeast basin is limited to Queensway Bridge. Liquefaction and settlement severely restrict rail access, and damage many rail-mounted gravity cranes.

Utility lines, oil pipelines, and waste water lines are extensively damaged, reducing the harbor operations to 25% for one week.

Fires occur in the harbor area; these and ruptured oil storage facilities pose the threat of a major fire.

Oscillatory water waves in enclosed bodies of water have damaged ships and moorings in the harbor areas from Santa Monica to Newport Beach.

Communications

Within 25 miles of the NIFZ, telephone lines designated for essential services are 25% usable in the first day, 50% usable in the second day, and 75% usable at the end of the third day. The availability of telephone communications for the public is significantly lower.

Electric Power Facilities

Five power plants: Harbor, Long Beach, Alamitos, Haynes, and Huntington Beach are shut down for more than 3 days. A post-earthquake inspection at the San Onofre nuclear power plant indicates no damage.

Five major transmission substations in the Culver City-Compton area are out of service for more than three days, making it difficult to reroute power into the area.

The 3 major substations serving coastal Orange County are out of service for more than 3 days, making it difficult to reroute power into the area.

Water Supply

The principal treatment plants in Los Angeles County, at El Segundo and Carson, are damaged and operate at less than 50% capacity. The main Orange County plant is in the NIFZ north of Newport Beach and is severely damaged; it will be inoperable for several months.

Main waste water lines in to the Carson treatment from the north (San Gabriel Valley) and the east (Long Beach) are heavily damaged at the fault crossing between Compton and Long Beach.

Damage and lack of fresh water for treatment and of electrical power for pumping, results in sewage flowing into soils, channels, and streets, contaminating the ground water and the coastline.

Natural Gas

Along the NIFZ there are thousands of damaged mains, valves, and service connections. There are numerous fires in streets at broken gas lines, and in structures at broken house line connections. Faulting causes breaks in major transmission pipelines at three locations: Slauson Avenue, 104th Street, and along the Los Angeles River.

Ground failures cause breaks in transmission lines in Sepulveda Canyon and Marina Del Rey.

In Long Beach Harbor the trunk line crossing at the Heim Bridge is broken due to ground failure.

The high pressure gas line to Huntington Beach power plant breaks where it crosses the marshlands east of Bolsa Chica State Park.

Petroleum

A major fire rages for several days at one of the refineries in the Carson-Wilmington area.

Many fuel lines rapture at the fault crossings, between Baldwin Hills and Huntington Beach.

In Los Angeles Harbor, ground failures rupture oil pipelines and storage facilities, discharging oil into the Channel. A fire on the Mormon Island poses the threat of a major conflagration.

The fuel line to LADWP's power plant in East Long Beach is ruptured by faulting.

In Seal Beach, ground failures have damaged storage facilities and piping, with consequent fuel spillage into Alamitos Bay.

The fuel line to Huntington Beach Power Plant is damaged by faulting.

FEDERAL AND STATE
EMERGENCY MANAGEMENT AGENCIES LIST

FEMA Headquarters
Federal Emergency Agency
500 C Street SW
Washington, DC 20472
(202)646-2500

FEMA Regional Offices
Region 1: Boston
(617)223-9540

Region 2: New York
(212)225-7209

Region 3: Philadelphia
(215)931-5500

Region 4: Atlanta
(404)853-4200

Region 5: Chicago
(312)408-5500

Region 6: Denton, TX
(817)898-5104

Region 7: Kansas City, MO
(816)283-7061

Region 8: Denver
(303)235-1813

Region 9: San Francisco
(415)923-7100

Region 10: Bothell, WA
(206)487-4604

STATE EMERGENCY MANAGEMENT AGENCIES
(FEMA REGION NUMBERS ARE IN PARENTHESES.)

Alabama (4)
Alabama Emergency Management
Agency
5898 S. County Road
Clanton, AL 35045
(205)280-2200

Alaska (10)
Division of Emergency Services
New Anchorage Armory
Fort Richardson
Bldg. 49000, Suite B-210
Fort Richardson, AK 99595-5750
(907)428-7000

Arkansas (6)
Office of Emergency Services
PO Box 758
Conway, AR 72032
(501)329-5601

California (9)
Office of Emergency Services
2800 Meadowview Rd.
Sacramento, CA 95823
(916)427-4990

Colorado (8)
Colorado Office of Emergency
Management
Camp George West
Golden, CO 80401
(303)273-1622

Connecticut (1)
Connecticut Office of Emergency
Management
360 Broad St.
Hartford, CT 06105
(203)566-3180

Delaware (3)
Division of Emergency Planning
& Operations
PO Box 527
Delaware City, DE 19706
(302)834-4531

District of Columbia (3)
Office of Emergency Preparedness
200 14th St., NW, 8th Floor
Washington, DC 20009
(202)727-3150

Florida (4)
Division of Emergency
Management
2740 Crestview Dr.
Tallahassee, FL 32399
(904)488-1900

Georgia
Georgia Emergency Management
Agency
PO Box 18055
Atlanta, GA 30316-0055
(404)624-7205

Hawaii (9)
State Civil Defense
3949 Diamond Head Road
Honolulu, HI 96816-4495
(808)734-2161

Idaho (10)
Bureau of Disaster Services
650 W. State St.
Boise, ID 83720
(208)334-3460

Illinois (5)
Illinois Emergency Management
Agency
110 E. Adams Street
Springfield, IL 62706
(217)782-2700

Indiana (5)
Indiana Emergency Management
Agency
State Office Bldg., Room E-208
302 W. Washington St.
Indianapolis, IN 46204
(317)232-3830

Iowa (7)
Iowa Emergency Management
Division
Hoover State Office Bldg.
Level A, Room 29
Des Moines, IA 50319
(515)281-3231

Kansas (7)
Division of Emergency
Preparedness
PO Box C300
Topeka, KS 66601
(913)266-1400

Kentucky (4)
Kentucky Disaster and Emergency
Services
Boone Center, Parkside Dr.
Frankfort, KY 40601
(502)564-8682

Louisiana (6)
Office of Emergency Preparedness
Department of Public Safety
LA Military Dept.
PO Box 44217
Capitol Station
Baton Rouge, LA 70804
(504)342-5470

Maine (1)
Maine Emergency Management
Agency
State Office Bldg, Station 72
August, ME 04333
(207)289-4080

Maryland (3)
Maryland Emergency
Management and
Civil Defense Agency
Two Sudbrook Ln., East
Pikesville, MD 21208
(301)486-4422

Massachusetts (1)
Massachusetts Emergency
Management Division

Michigan
Michigan State Police
300 S. Washington So.
Suite 300
Lansing, MI 48913
(517)334-5130

Minnesota (5)
Division of Emergency Services
Department of Public Safety
State Capitol, B-5
St. Paul, MN 55155
(612)296-2233

Mississippi (4)
Mississippi Emergency
Management Agency
PO Box 4501, Fondren Station
Jackson, MS 39296
(601)352-9100

Missouri (7)
State Emergency Management
Agency
PO Box 116
Jefferson City, MO 65102
(314)751-9779

Montana (8)
Emergency Management Specialist
Disaster and Emergency Services
PO Box 4789
Helena, MT 59604-4789
(406)444-6911

Nebraska
Nebraska Civil Defense Agency
National Guard Center
1300 Military Road
Lincoln, NE 68508-1090
(402)473-1410

Nevada (9)
Nevada Division of Emergency
Services
2525 S. Carson St.
Carson City, NV 89710
(702)887-7302

New Hampshire (1)
Governor's Office of Emergency
Management
State Office Park South
107 Pleasant St
Concord, NH 03301
(603)271-2231

New Jersey (2)
Office of Emergency Management
PO Box 7068
W. Trenton, NJ 08628-0068
(609)538-6050

New Mexico (6)
Emergency Planning and
Coordination
Dept. of Public Safety
4491 Cerrillos Road
PO Box 1628
Santa Fe, NM 85704
(505)827-9222

New York (2)
State Emergency Management
Office
Public Security Building #22
State Campus
Albany, NY 12226-5000
(518)457-2222

North Carolina
Division of Emergency
Management
116 West Jones St.
Raleigh, NC 27603-1335
(919)733-3867

North Dakota(8)
North Dakota Division of
Emergency Management
PO Box 5511
Bismarck, ND 58502-5511
(701)224-2113

Ohio
Ohio Emergency Management
Agency
2825 W. Granville Road
Columbus, OH 43235-2712
(614)889-7150

Oklahoma (6)
Oklahoma Civil Defense
PO Box 53365
Oklahoma City, OK 73152
(405)521-2481

Oregon (10)
Emergency Management Division
Oregon State Executive
Department
595 Cottage St., NE
Salem, OR 97310
(503)378-4124

Pennsylvania (3)
Pennsylvania Emergency
Management Agency
PO Box 3321
Harrisburg, PA 17105-3321
(717)783-8016

Puerto Rico (2)
State Civil Defense
Commonwealth of Puerto Rico
PO Box 5127
San Juan, PR 00906
(809)724-0124

Rhode Island
Rhode Island Emergency
Management Agency
State House, Room 27
Providence, RI 02903
(401)421-7333

South Carolina
South Carolina Emergency
Management Division
1429 Senate St., Rutledge Bldg.
Columbia, SC 29201-3782
(803)734-8020

South Dakota (4)
Division of Emergency and
Disaster Services
State Capitol, 500 East Capitol
Pierre, SD 57501
(605)773-3231

Tennessee (4)
Tennessee Emergency
Management Agency
3041 Sidco Dr.
Nashville, TN 37204-1502
(615)741-0001

Texas (6)
Division of Emergency
Management
PO Box 4087
Austin, TX 78773-4087
(512)465-2183

Utah (8)
Division of Comprehensive
Emergency Management
State Office Bldg., Room 1110
Salt Lake City, UT 84114
(801)538-3400

Vermont (1)
Vermont Emergency Management
Agency
Dept. of Public Safety
Waterbury State Complex
103 S. Main St.
Waterbury, VT 05676
(802)244-8271

Virgin Islands (2)
Office of Civil Defense and
Emergency Services
131 Gallows Bay
Christiansted, VI 00820
(809)773-2244

Virginia (3)
Department of Emergency
Services
310 Turner Road
Richmond, VA 23225-6491
(804)674-2497

Washington (10)
Division of Emergency
Management
4220 E. Martin Way, MS-PT 11
Olympia, WA 98504-8346
(206)923-4901

West Virginia (3)
West Virginia Office of
Emergency Services
State Capitol Complex
Room EB80
Charleston, WV 25305
(304)558-5380

Wisconsin (5)
Division of Emergency
Government
4802 Sheboygan Ave., Room 99A
Madison, WI 53707
(608)266-3232

Wyoming (8)
Wyoming Emergency
Management Agency
PO Box 1709
Cheyenne, WY 82003
(307)777-7566

VULNERABILITY ANALYSIS WORKSHEET

TYPE OF EMERGENCY	Probability High Low 5 ↔ 1	Human Impact High	Property Impact Impact 5	Business Impact 1	Environmental Impact Low Impact	Internal Resources Weak Resources 5	External Resources Strong Resources 1	Total

The lower the score the better

Appendix X

TRAINING AND DRILL EXERCISES WORKSHEET

	JAN	FEB	MAR	APRIL	MAY	JUNE	JULY	AUG	SEPT	OCT	NOV	DEC
MANAGEMENT ORIENTATION/ REVIEW												
EMPLOYEE ORIENTATION/ REVIEW												
CONTRACTOR ORIENTATION/ REVIEW												
COMMUNITY/MEDIA ORIENTATION /REVIEW												
MANAGEMENT TABLETOP EXERCISE												
RESPONSE TEAM TABLETOP EXERCISE												
WALK-THROUGH DRILL												
FUNCTIONAL DRILLS												
EVACUATION DRILL												
FULL-SCALE EXERCISE												

Appendix Y

INTERNET ADDRESSES:
ENVIRONMENTAL/PRECIOUS METALS LIST

Environmental Agencies

Australia Environment Protection Agency
http://kaos.erin.gov.au/portfolio/epa/epa.html

California Environmental Protection Agency (Cal-EPA)
http://www.cahwnet.gov/epa/

Environment Canada: The Green Lane
http://www.doe.ca/
> Comments: Parallel English and French versions. This site won: "Best Canadian Government Web Site, 1995"

Great Britain Department of the Environment
http://www.open.gov.uk/doe/doehome.htm

Ohio Environmental Protection Agency
http://www.epa.ohio.gov/
> Comments: Average number of 1996 requests for this popular information source (January-March): 209/hr., 5,033/day, 181,856 total.

United Nations Environment Programme (Switzerland)
http://www.unep.ch/
> Comments: Includes "hot-link" to *Basel Convention on the Control of Transboundary Movements of Hazardous Wastes and their Disposal* (http://www.unep.ch/sbc.html).

United States Environmental Protection Agency (EPA)
http://www.epa.gov/
> Comments: EPA's main Homepage is the starting point for finding the U.S. government's vast computer resources on environmental regulation. Includes daily updates of the Federal Register and access to the entire U.S. Code and Code of Federal Regulations (C.F.R.).

Banks

Mizrahi Bank, International Client Services
http://www.mizrahi.com/html/int-deal.htm
>   Comments: Mizrahi is a trader of currencies, precious metals, options
>   and other financial instruments.

Exchanges

Dallas Gold & Silver Exchange
http://www.iminet.com/jewelry/bullion.html
>   Comments: Dallas Gold & Silver Exchange, a public company, trades
>   precious metals. The site includes the *Computer Jewelry Exchange*,
>   where jewelry buyers and sellers from all over the world meet on the
>   Internet. For example, a seller in Switzerland sends a ring that he or
>   she thinks is worth $1000. A buyer in New Jersey looks at the
>   description and picture and then decides that it is a good buy at $750.
>   The buyer registers and receives a bidder number and now has full
>   access to the "Trading Floor." The registered bidder then enters an
>   anonymous bid for $750. The owner can hold to $1000, lower the
>   offering price to come closer to the high bid amount, or they can "hit"
>   the bid and complete a transaction.

New York Mercantile Exchange
http://www.ino.com/gen/nymex/whatsnew.html
>   Comments: Includes free "real-audio" sounds of the trading floor. The
>   NYMEX is the world's largest physical commodity futures exchange,
>   and the preeminent trading forum for energy, precious metals, and, in
>   North America, copper.

Environmental Consultants

ATEC Associates, Inc.
http://www.atecengr.com

Geraghty & Miller
http://www.gmgw.com
>   Comments: One of America's premiere groundwater consultants. The
>   site offers detailed operational capabilities and newsletter ordering on-
>   line.

Harding Lawson Associates
http://www.harding.com

Investments

Canadian Mutual Fund Tables
http://www.visions.com/mutuals/req/req.html
> Comments: Published by Southam Inc., includes updated rates and
> returns for funds such as FCMI Precious Metals, Royal Precious
> Metals, Altamira Precious Metals, and Green Line Precious Metals.

Dynamic Mutual Funds
http://www.dynamic.ca/test/dynprecmet.html
> Comments: Dynamic Precious Metals Fund portfolio explanations
> (e.g., precious metals companies and gold/platinum bullion and
> short-term notes).

Information Line (International Financial Consultants Inc.)
http://www.intelweb.com/infopass.htm
> Comments: Consultants and broker/dealers in precious metals.

Fidelity Select Precious Metals and Minerals Portfolio Monthly NAV History
http://www.fid-inv.com/mutual/fund_data/ST/61_mkt.html
> Comments: Produced by Fidelity Investors, Online Investor Services,
> NAV is through the last Friday of the month, adjusted for reinvestment
> of capital gains and dividends.

Monex Deposit Company, Monex Credit Company
http://www.calypso.com/monex/index.html
> Comments: Precious metals investments for the individual investor.

Stock Room
http://loft-gw.zone.org/jason/GOLD.html
> Comments: While only one page, enjoyable up-to-date graphics on
> gold and silver prices. Huge response, with "counter" showing 205,000
> "visitors" to site for last six months of 1995.

Law Firms (Environmental/Precious Metals)

Brown, Pistone, Hurley & Van Vlear
http://www.jdlist.com/bp/
> Comments: A professional law corporation, founded in 1989 and based
> in Irvine, California, emphasizes construction, environmental, and
> technology law. Features practice area summaries and attorney
> pictures/biographies.

Mining

Northern Miner
http://www.scis.southam.com/northernminer/home.html
> Comments: Weekly newspaper covering the activities of North American-based mining companies. The current issue is on line, and extensive "hot-links" to mining publications. Content includes exploration results, onsite reports, company profiles, international projects.

Precious Metals Companies

Chugoku Kogyo, Chemical-Metal Department
http://www.chemical-metal.co.jp/cgk/cm.html
> Comments: The company sells non-ferrous metals and precious metals and does reclamation of scraps of rare metals.

Goldtek
http://www.village.com/business/goldtek.html
> Comments: Reclaimers of gold, silver and platinum from electronic components.

Johnson Matthey
http://www.eznet.com/jme/jmhp.htm
> Comments: This service, updated daily, includes in depth data on all Johnson Matthey products, access to customer service groups, a listing of new products, an overview of current R&D projects.

Kitco Inc.
http://www.kitco.com/gold.hotlink.html
> Comments: Internet "hotlink" page for precious metals industry. On-line Assay Result and Metal Credit: Customers can retrieve refining results 24 hrs. per day, with all metal credits and charges displayed. They will execute settlement options at the start of the next business day.

Mitsui USA
http://204.119.191.135/mitdept.html

Pyramid Precious
http://www.dircon.co.uk/xxx/pyramid/index.htm
> Comments: British gold, silver and platinum precious metals recovery.

Remco Engineering
http://www.remco.com./~remcobob/gold.htm
> Comments: The Remco Engineering Gold recovery ion exchange module, for gold rinses, uses multiple columns to provide a long path length and a long residence time in a compact unit.

Reynolds Metals Company, Raw Materials/Precious Metals Division
http://www.rmc.com/divs/rawprec.html
> Comments: Incomplete, "under construction" as of January 1996.

Royal Canadian Mint
http://www.rcmint.ca/cgi-bin/imagemap/rcm.map?41,20
> Comments: The Royal Canadian Mint is a Crown corporation that produces coin and coin related products for domestic and international markets. Established in 1908, the Mint is known worldwide as a top provider of circulation coins, numismatic products, and bullion.

Selket Precious Metals, Inc.
http://www.kern.com/~cwmarket/biz/selket/selket.html
> Comments: Selket has mines in Oregon with considerable gold, silver and other metal reserves.

Trelleborg Group
http://www.trellgroup.se/trellgroup/
> Comments: The Trelleborg Group, is a 90 year old Swedish conglomerate handling precious metals, with 42% of its sales in Sweden, 35% in the EC, and 12% in the U.S./Canada.

Reference/Misc.

Argonne National Laboratory
http://www.anl.gov/
> Comments: Argonne National Laboratory's the first national laboratory and one of the U.S. Department of Energy's largest energy research centers, with an annual operating budget of about $490 million supporting more than 200 research projects.

ArtMetal Resource To Metalworking
http://wuarchive.wustl.edu/edu/arts/metal/AM_res.html
> Comments: To serve those interested in the various aspects of working artistically with metals, the ArtMetal Project is a collection of metalworking resources, including specific references to non-ferrous precious metals.

ASTM
http://www.astm.org
>Comments: Organized in 1898, ASTM (the American Society for
Testing and Materials), writes standards for materials, products,
systems, and services. Also available are other standards, e.g.,
International Standards Organization (ISO) 14000 Series on
"Environmental Management Draft International Standards &
Committee Draft Standards."

Browse by Industry
http://cyberplex.com/CyberPlex/ARS/BrowseIndustry.html
>Comments: Instant on-line ordering of annual reports. Browse by
industry groupings or Standard Industry Codes (SIC's), including
"Precious Metals."

Galaxy (Metals & Minerals)
http://www.einet.net:8000/galaxy/Business-and-Commerce/General-Products-an
d-Services/Metals-and-Minerals.html
>Comments: General Products and Services related to Metals and
Minerals, including precious metals.

Greenpeace International
http://www.greenpeace.org
>Comments: Whatever one's political views, Greenpeace's numbers are
impressive at their Amsterdam main Homepage: 496,402 visits as a
one week 1995 high; 305,511 during the week of March 17-24, 1996.

Periodic Table
http://www-c8.lanl.gov/infosys/html/periodic/periodic-main.html
>Comments: Los Alamos National Laboratory has established a simple
point-and-click periodic table which "hot-links" the user to history and
technical data on all periodic elements, including precious metals.

Preventive Dental Association
http://204.250.87.46/P/PDHA/email/gold.htm
>Comments: Review on preference for noble alloys gold and platinum,
with avoidance of nickel, palladium, copper, beryllium and cobalt.
Mentions brand names such as Degussa G and Argident 88 as high
gold, low toxicity metals.

Prospecting Page
http://www.worldspan.net/~infosvc/treasure/html/prospct2.html
> Comments: The authors devote this site to individuals in search of precious metal in its raw form. Whether it is gold, silver or even something as unusual as uranium, one can find information related to the search at this site.

Recycler's World, Associations Listing
http://granite.sentex.net/recycle/Associations/rs000113.html
> Comments: Lists associations about recycling, including name and address of International Precious Metals Institute (IPMI).

TMS (Minerals, Metals & Materials Society) Membership Application
http://www.tms.org/Society/MembershipApp.html
> Comments: The mission of TMS is to promote the science and engineering professions concerned with minerals, metals and materials.

INDEX

acid 32, 131

agency   2, 10, 18, 19, 22, 23, 27, 48-54, 58, 59, 72, 74, 81, 120, 146, 152

amber list 46, 47

attorney confidentiality 69, 80, 98

audit 68, 80-82, 84, 98, 127

audits 80, 127

Austria 47, 48

bankruptcy 64, 89-92

Basel Convention 6, 43-46

Bhopal 23, 115, 128

Brazil 48

British Act 48-54

Brownfields 55, 65-68

California .   6, 10, 31, 37, 55-60, 62, 72, 77, 81, 82, 85, 87, 95, 115-119,
                                                   138, 141, 143, 152-154

catalyst 1, 8, 152

catalysts 8, 46, 152

CERCLA   . . .   2, 16, 17, 24, 25, 29-40, 47, 48, 50, 51, 53, 61, 78, 91-93,
                                                        102, 152, 154

certification 95, 106, 112

CGL policy 83

Clean Air Act 2, 13, 31, 63

Clean Water Act 2, 12, 13, 15, 22

cleanup   2, 17, 29, 32, 33, 35, 36, 40, 47, 50, 55, 56, 59, 61, 63, 65, 67,
               70-73, 78, 80, 84, 86, 90, 92, 93, 99, 102, 110, 133, 135,
                                                                      136

cleanups 33, 49, 55, 66, 68, 103, 154

community right-to-know 23, 24, 26

computer 2, 6, 9, 143-146, 153-155

consultant 71-74, 87, 128, 142

contamination   . 33, 38, 40, 41, 48, 54, 56, 57, 60, 64, 65, 68, 70-74, 78,
                                                    83, 95, 100, 122, 144

copper 4, 7, 8, 12, 32, 44

corporate veil 77, 79

criminal 15, 16, 22, 29, 77, 81, 105

cyanides 3, 25, 32, 44

Denmark 47, 48

director 18, 56, 152, 154

directors . . . . 77, 78, 152 disaster . . . 1, 23, 115-117, 119, 120, 124, 125, 128, 130-132, 134, 135, 138, 142-144, 153

disasters 115, 119, 141, 142

disposal . 1, 10, 13, 14, 16, 18, 29-31, 35, 36, 38-40, 43, 44, 64, 78, 80, 84, 88, 95, 99, 101, 102

earthquake 116, 118, 119, 125, 137-144

earthquakes 115, 121, 123, 137, 141-143

electronic scrap 9, 45, 46

emergency 15, 23-26, 111, 115, 119-128, 130, 131, 134, 136, 141, 142

enforcement 2, 15, 27, 59, 81, 91

EPA 2, 4, 5, 10, 13-22, 24, 26, 27, 29, 32-34, 38-40, 47, 51, 59, 68, 81, 82, 85, 95, 109, 111, 113

Europe 43, 115, 128, 129

exception report 113

exemption 11, 15, 17-19, 25, 55, 65, 105, 107

experts 47, 68, 119, 120, 128, 133, 135, 138, 139

export 16, 44-47

fine 2, 16, 23, 27, 29

fines 16, 23, 27, 29, 51, 103, 122

fire 62, 117-120, 123, 124, 130-132, 134, 135, 142, 143, 153

fires 115, 118, 121, 123, 130-132, 142

flood 115, 118, 132-136

floods 115, 123, 132, 133

generator 15, 18, 19, 21, 95, 102, 110-113, 142

generators . . 11, 14, 15, 17, 18, 20, 21, 85, 95, 105, 109, 110, 112, 113, 136

Germany 6, 45, 47, 48

gold 3, 4, 6, 7, 19, 38, 39, 106

green list 46

hazardous material 105-110, 121, 142

hazardous materials 1, 59, 80, 100, 101, 105-110, 117, 119-121, 123

hazardous waste . . . 8, 10, 11, 13-17, 19, 21, 29, 31, 38-40, 47, 68, 71, 77, 83, 85, 88, 90, 92, 93, 95-104, 106, 109-111, 113, 152

hazardous wastes . 11, 13-19, 21, 30, 38, 39, 43, 46, 47, 78, 88, 99, 103, 109, 110

insurance 29, 67, 74, 80, 82-88, 95, 118, 120, 133

interim status 14, 15

international 1-3, 5, 6, 16, 31, 37, 43, 45, 110, 112, 128, 143, 152, 153

Internet 3, 4, 145, 146, 154

inventory 24, 26, 27, 68, 98-100, 133

IPMI 5, 6, 9, 10, 17, 18, 23, 31, 38, 43, 45-47, 106, 145, 146, 152, 155

iridium 4, 19

Japan 47, 48, 115, 118, 138, 146
jewelry 7, 8, 10-12, 38
Kobe 115, 118, 138
labeling 105
Lawrence Livermore National Laboratory 56
lead 3, 4, 7, 12, 32, 44, 59, 60, 85, 126, 141
liability . 2, 15, 17, 23, 29, 31, 35-41, 45, 47, 48, 52, 55, 60, 64, 67, 68,
      70, 71, 77-86, 88-91, 93, 95, 102, 110, 118, 119, 152
Love Canal 29
manifest 11, 16, 95, 109-113
manifests 10, 100, 110
media 43, 124, 125, 128, 129
mercury 4, 10, 32, 40
mine 3, 55
minimization 1, 15, 87, 95-98, 102, 104, 112
Mississippi 115, 118, 135, 138
Monsanto 135-137
N.C.P. 30, 32-34, 50
National Response Center 25, 30
Netherlands 47, 48
New Jersey 59, 63-66, 92
Nissan 141, 142
Northridge 115, 125, 138, 139, 143
nuisance 36, 60-62, 117
OECD 44-47
officer 85
officers 15, 23, 77, 78
operator 25, 34, 35, 62, 71, 102, 112
operators 24, 26, 30, 48, 63, 85, 88, 112
osmium 4, 19
owner 25, 30, 34, 35, 53, 60, 62, 71, 80, 85, 112, 118
owners . 24, 26, 29, 48, 53, 60, 63, 67, 68, 70, 85, 88, 130, 132, 133, 141
packaging 9, 105-107, 110, 137
palladium 3, 4, 8, 19, 152
parent corporation 78
PCB's 10, 72
Pennsylvania 1, 5, 62, 63
petroleum exclusion 17, 35
Phase I 69, 70, 72, 84
pipeline 30, 141
platinum 3, 4, 19, 152
precious metal 4, 9, 11, 18, 19, 21, 31, 37-40, 46

precious metals 1-6, 8-10, 12, 13, 17-21, 25, 37, 44-47, 55,
106, 111, 145, 146, 152, 154
precious metals-bearing 2, 3, 6, 17, 44, 45
RCRA 8, 10, 13-21, 47, 53, 61, 88, 109, 112, 152
reclaimer 18, 21, 110
reclaimers 9, 10, 18-21
records retention 113
recycle 17, 102
recycling 5, 6, 10, 14, 17, 18, 20, 21, 37, 44, 102, 111
refiner 38, 39
refiners 5, 9, 152
refinery customers 31, 37, 38
release   17, 21, 24-26, 30-32, 40, 52, 53, 59, 90, 101, 102, 108, 115, 128,
142
releases 23, 25, 29, 35, 82, 83, 96, 119, 123, 142
response plan 122, 126, 141, 142
rhodium 4, 19
risk management 1, 77, 79, 80, 89, 98, 118, 154
risk-based corrective action 56, 58
Rocketdyne 143, 144
ruthenium 4, 19
safety 10, 26, 48, 59, 82, 100, 115-118, 121, 123, 153
secondary market 2, 6, 44-46, 111
shareholder 67, 78
shareholders 77, 78, 125
shipping papers 109
silver 3, 4, 7, 12, 19, 21, 31, 40
Single Agency Designation 59
small quantity 11, 14, 95, 108, 112
solid waste 13, 14, 17, 22, 31
storage   10, 13, 14, 16, 18, 19, 21, 24, 30, 56, 64, 73, 80, 85, 88, 98, 100,
116, 118, 132-134, 141
strict liability 35, 36, 48
subsidiary 78, 79
tank 56, 58, 85, 130, 141
tanks 25, 73, 85, 116, 118, 119, 134, 135, 140, 141
toxic 10, 11, 21, 24, 26, 31, 44, 99, 115, 123, 142
toxicity 8, 10, 11, 14, 15, 33, 95, 99, 112
training 13, 80, 96, 121, 122, 125-127, 136, 142, 143, 154
transaction 65, 70
transportation 8, 9, 13, 14, 16, 18, 25, 37, 64, 78, 85, 95, 102, 105,
106, 108, 110, 111, 117, 121, 125
trespass 62
trial 36, 75, 154
Union Carbide 128, 129

vulnerability assessment 120
zinc 7, 12, 32, 44

BOOK TEAM PROFILES

J.P. Rosso (Director of Publishing)

Julia E. Kress, Esq. (Contributing Author)

Michael Paul Hutchins, Esq., P.E., R.D.S.W. (Contributing Author)

John E. Van Vlear, Esq., R.E.A. (Author)

BOOK TEAM PROFILES

J.P. Rosso (Director of Publishing)

Mr. Rosso is the Vice President for Marketing and Administration and Director at Gemini Industries in Santa Ana, California, directing the Marketing Department for 15 years. Mr. Rosso is the 1996-97 President of the International Precious Metals Institute, having served for five years on the IPMI Board of Directors. He is also Gemini's representative to the National Petroleum Refiners Association.

Gemini Industries, founded in 1973, provides precious metals recovery and refining services to petroleum and chemical catalyst users. Privately owned by the original founders, Gemini is the largest processor of the recovery of platinum, rhenium, and palladium from spent petroleum reforming, isomerization and chemical catalysts. The company uses advanced technology and specialization in catalyst processing, which enables it to offer competitive prices and metal return schedules. Gemini's technical support and analytical groups insure maximum accuracy and accountability in sampling, analysis, and evaluation. Strict environmental controls insure zero discharge and complete treatment of liquids, solids and gases. Gemini's clients have no possible long term liability associated with wastes.

Mr. Rosso received his degree from Loyola University in Los Angeles (B.A. 1975). His graduate work includes studies at Whittier College School of Law, and M.B.A. programs at California State University, Long Beach and University of Redlands.

Mr. Rosso can be reached by his direct telephone/voice mail (714/250-4011 x.229).

Julia E. Kress, Esq. (Contributing Author)

Ms. Kress is an environmental lawyer with Brown, Pistone, Hurley & Van Vlear, in Irvine, CA where she practices environmental litigation and compliance. Ms. Kress' experience includes litigation, real property transactions, site assessment and remediation, and agency reporting and permitting. Her practice includes knowledge of most federal and state statutes and regulations concerning solid and hazardous waste management, air quality, and water quality (including RCRA, CERCLA, OSHA, federal and California Clean Air Acts, Proposition 65, CEQA, and Air Toxics "Hot Spots" Act).

Ms. Kress has been involved in CERCLA ("Superfund") litigation involving contaminated sites. She also has participated in many hearings, appeals, and settlement negotiations with federal, state, and local environmental agencies.

Ms. Kress earned her degree in Business Administration, with a major in Finance, from Loyola University of Chicago (B.A. 1988) and Law Degree from Loyola Law School (J.D. 1991). She is currently a member of the Los Angeles and Orange County Bar Associations and the Women's Environmental Council.

Ms. Kress can be reached by her direct telephone/voice mail (714/450-8429) or by computer e-mail (Jules82266@aol.com).

Michael Paul Hutchins, Esq., P.E., R.D.S.W. (Contributing Author)

Mr. Hutchins is a construction, environmental, and technology lawyer with Brown, Pistone, Hurley & Van Vlear. His litigation experience includes contract disputes, construction delays, product defects, and environmental cost recovery and site remediation. Mr. Hutchins is also active in contract negotiations, patents and trademarks, and plan and specification variances.

Before joining Brown, Pistone, Hurley & Van Vlear, Mr. Hutchins practiced engineering for eight years in the manufacturing and construction industries. His work included product development, profit and loss responsibility, and project management throughout the United States for a Fortune 500 company.

Mr. Hutchins is a registered Civil Engineer in California and Washington, and a California Registered Disaster Service Worker in structural safety assessments. He is a member of the American Association of Civil Engineers, the National Fire Protection Association and the International Conference of Building Officials. Mr. Hutchins has spoken to public utilities and seminar groups on product design and performance and construction techniques. He has written manufacturing and performance specifications and an analysis of the landmark California Supreme Court Decision Montrose Chemical Corp. v. Admiral Ins., *The Law Report*, August 1995.

Education: Mr. Hutchins earned his undergraduate degree from Villanova University (B.S.C.E. 1984, Chi Epsilon) and his law degree from University of Minnesota School of Law (J.D. 1993).

Mr. Hutchins can be reached by his direct telephone/voice mail (714/450-8433).

John E. Van Vlear, Esq., R.E.A.
(Author)

Mr. Van Vlear is Chair of the Environmental Practice for Brown, Pistone, Hurley & Van Vlear. The professional law corporation, founded in 1989 and based in Irvine, California, emphasizes construction, environmental, and technology law. Mr. Van Vlear serves as environmental counselor, trial attorney, and strategy-level project manager on site cleanups, property transfers, risk management, and operations. He is a California Registered Environmental Assessor (R.E.A.) and a member of the California Bar.

Mr. Van Vlear teaches (e.g., former Adjunct Professor of Environmental Law at Western State University College of Law) and is a frequent public speaker. He is co-chair of the Orange County Bar Association's Environmental Law Section. From 1991-1994, Mr. Van Vlear served as Founding President of the non-profit Environmental Professionals Organization ("EPO"), continuing to serve after that as its Executive Director. Since 1985, he has published extensively, including: a book section on environmental strategies for the precious metals industry, articles on CERCLA, financing cleanups, and handling environmental consultants, and an award-winning law review article on land use aesthetics.

Education: University of California at Irvine, Social Ecology (B.A. 1984, *magna cum laude*, Phi Beta Kappa), Pepperdine University School of Law (J.D. 1987, *cum laude*). Mr. Van Vlear has graduate-level training in environmental sampling techniques, computer groundwater modeling, and remediation system design.

Mr. Van Vlear encourages all inquiries and can be reached at his direct telephone/voice mail (714/450-8435) or secondarily by Internet computer e-mail (*VanVlear@aol.com*).